OLIVE

CHARLES DICKENS

Stage 5

Retold by Catherine Skliarova

GET IT ON Google Play

Download on the App Store

Sesli kütüphanemize yukarıdaki karekodu okutarak veya Google Play / App Store üzerinden MK Publications yazarak ulaşabilirsiniz.

MK PUBLICATIONS

MK PUBLICATIONS

MK Publications Yayıncılık Ltd. Şti.
MK Plaza, Ferhatpaşa Mah. 22. Sk. No.50
34888 Ataşehir / İstanbul
Tel : +90 (216) 469 50 15
Web : www.mkpublications.com.tr
e-mail : info@mkpublications.com.tr

ISBN: 978-605-9533-70-6
Sertifika No: 47283
FIFTH EDITION – OCTOBER 2023

Author: Charles Dickens
Retold by: Catherine Skliarova
Series Editor: Murat Kurt
Cover and Page Design: Ibrahim Mısır
Picture Researcher: Burak Kurt
Cover Photograph: iStockphoto

Printed in Istanbul
Unifset Basım Yayın San. ve Tic. Ltd. Şti.
Kavaklı Mah. 57 Alay Sok. No: 14 B
34520 Beylikdüzü / İSTANBUL
Tel: +90 (212) 875 37 85
www.unifset.com
Sertifika: 72541

Contents

Chapter 1

Oliver Twist's Birth And Growth

One day, a boy was born in a small workhouse whose name is prefixed to the head of this chapter. For a long time, it was doubtful whether the baby would survive to bear any name at all. The thing is the baby found it difficult to breathe. It lay on the mattress, waiting silently between this world and the other. There was nobody nearby, but a poor old woman and a simple doctor. Oliver and Nature both won the fight. The result was that Oliver breathed and cried loudly on the mattress. A pale young woman rose weakly from the pillow and asked the doctor to show her new-born baby to her. The doctor gave it to her arms. She kissed its forehead with her white lips, looked at it happily, and then died. The doctor took the baby and put it back to the mattress.

"Who was his mother?" asked the doctor.

"I brought her here last night," answered the old woman. "She had walked some distance. Her shoes were worn to pieces. Nobody knows where she came from or where she was going."

"I understand. Please, look after the child and feed him with milk. Good-bye!" said the doctor, walking out of the room.

The old woman sat down by the fire and began to dress the baby. She wrapped it in the old fabrics which had become yellow with time. Thus he held his place within society – the orphan of the workhouse. The baby was called Oliver Twist. Oliver cried loudly. If he could have known that he was an orphan, perhaps he would cry even louder. The next day Oliver

Twist was sent to another house, in which many orphans lived under the control of an old greedy woman. She knew what was good for children, and she had a very good idea of what was good to her. So, she spent the greater part of the money (the money was sent to her every week by the authorities) to her own use. That is why Oliver tried to live on the smallest possible portion of food very desperately. He was the victim of systematic treachery. That is more; he was brought up mostly by hand. The greedy woman, Mrs Mann, beat Oliver and other orphans very often, considering her beating a very important part of education. Of course, this system of education would never produce any extraordinary crop. Oliver Twist was a very thin and pale child at his nine years old. But he had a strong spirit in his breast, which grew stronger day by day despite Mrs Mann's strict diet. One day, Mr Bumble visited Mrs Mann in her orphan house. Mr Bumble was a government official who took care of all orphans in the workhouses. Mrs Mann greeted him kindly at the gate and led him into the house. As they entered the house, she put a chair for him to sit and looked at him attentively.

"Oliver Twist is nine years old already," said Mr Bumble. "We could not discover his parents. Anyway, Oliver is too old to remain here. I came here to take him and bring him back to the workhouse."

Mrs Mann left the room to bring Oliver at once. Soon Oliver stood before Mr Bumble, all confused and scared. But then the news of his immediate departure made him the happiest boy in the world. He did not feel great regret at going away. Thus Oliver left the miserable orphan house, where even one kind word had never been said to him. He followed Mr Bumble as quickly as he could. They reached the workhouse after one hour. Mr Bumble led him to the room, where a fat man was sitting at his table with a serious face. Oliver did not like this fat man. Mr Bumble gave him a tap behind which made him cry at once.

"Why are you crying?" asked the fat man. "I know you are an orphan. I hope you pray for the people who feed you and take care of you. Well, you have come here to be educated and taught a useful trade. You will live in this workhouse till we find some work for you."

Oliver made a bow silently and left the room with Mr Bumble. Thus Oliver began to live in the workhouse. The workhouse was a big and cold building, full of poor families and orphans. All that Oliver ate was a spoon of gruel and a small piece of bread twice a week. The dining-room was a large stone hall. A cooker, dressed in a grey apron, placed the gruel with a spoon to each of the plates. The bowls never needed washing. The boys polished them with their spoons till they shone again. Oliver was always hungry. After three months, Oliver was so hungry that he could hardly sleep at night. One day, one of the strongest boys proposed to ask for more gruel. He had so wild eyes that all the boys were afraid of him. Oliver Twist was chosen to walk to the cooker that evening and ask for more gruel. Presently, the evening arrived. The boys took their places as usual. The gruel was served out and finished rapidly. The boys winked at Oliver. Oliver was desperate with hunger and weak with misery. He rose from the table and walked up to the cooker, with a plate and a spoon in his hand.

"Please, sir, I want some more," said Oliver.

The cooker turned very pale with anger. He looked at Oliver in surprise. Oliver was paralysed with fear at that moment.

"What?" asked the cooker.

"Please, I want some more," repeated Oliver.

The cooker hit Oliver on the head with his spoon and cried aloud for the master of the workhouse. Soon Oliver was sent to the empty, cold room. The next morning, the master of the workhouse offered five pounds to anybody who would take Oliver as his apprentice to any trade. Thus a note was fastened to the gate of the workhouse, which informed of a young boy who could be an apprentice to any trade. Oliver remained a closed prisoner in the dark room for a week or so. He cried bitterly all day, and when the cold night came on he shut his eyes and tried to sleep. He walked every morning in a stone yard in the presence of Mr Bumble. As for society, he was carried every day into the hall when the boys dined. The cooker beat him mercilessly as a public warning and example. Oliver felt very ashamed and sad all the time. After two weeks, Mr Sowerberry read the note on the gate and entered the workhouse in order to talk about the apprentice he needed. He was a local coffin maker, who always was dressed in black suit and shoes. Mr Bumble met him at the entrance with a kind smile on his face. Oliver Twist was main thought in his mind at the time. He greeted Mr Sowerberry and shook his hand joyfully.

"Did you come here for an apprentice?" asked Mr Bumble.

"Yes," answered Mr Sowerberry. "I think I will take the boy. I need a good helper now."

Mr Bumble was beside himself with joy. He led Mr Sowerberry to the master of the workhouse and soon it was arranged that Oliver would go away that evening. The evening came quickly. Oliver stood silently before Mr Bumble at the entrance of the workhouse. He heard the news of his destination quite indifferently. Then he put on his old coat and left the workhouse with Mr Bumble, following him as obediently as a dog. Mr Bumble was to lead him to Mr Sowerberry's house and leave him there. As they walked on the street, Mr Bumble turned to Oliver and said:

"Well, of all the worst boys I have ever seen, you are …"

"No, no, sir!" cried Oliver. "I will be a good boy. I am a very little boy. And I feel so lonely. Everybody hates me. Please, don't be angry with me!"

Mr Bumble looked at him with some astonishment for a few seconds. Then he told him to walk faster. His cold heart could not understand Oliver's suffering and loneliness. After some time, they entered Mr Sowerberry's shop. Mr Sowerberry found Oliver too small and thin to be his apprentice. Nevertheless, after a short pause, he decided to take him and educate for his profession. He ordered him to go into a cellar and eat some cold meat as his supper. Oliver's eyes shone at the mention of the meat immediately. He went quickly to the cellar and found there some broken bones on a metal plate. He ate the remains of the meat that the dog had neglected with great joy. When Oliver finished his supper, Mr Sowerberry showed him his bed in the corner among the coffins and went away. Oliver went to his bed and closed his eyes at once, trying not to look at the unfinished coffins in the darkness. A cold fear came over him at that moment. He was alone in a strange place and had no friends to care for him. Actually, he had nobody who would love him or say a kind word to him. This thought made Oliver very sad and melancholy.

Chapter 2

Oliver Escapes To London

Oliver woke up in the morning by a loud kicking at the outside door. He jumped to his feet and ran up to the door as quickly as he could. As he opened the door, he saw a tall boy in the doorway who looked quite angrily at him.

"I think you do not know who I am," said the tall boy. "I am Noah Claypole, and I am your master. I work with Mr Sowerberry. So open the shutters, you lazy boy!"

Oliver opened the shutters straight away. Shortly afterwards, Mr Sowerberry appeared. He told Oliver to follow him down the stairs for breakfast. Oliver did so straight away. Mr Sowerberry's wife, Mrs Charlotte, gave Oliver a piece of bread and a cup of tea. Oliver finished his breakfast greedily. Noah mocked at him all the time, calling him a lonely workhouse orphan who had no friends. Noah was a bad boy. He was much older than Oliver. He was not a workhouse orphan, indeed. He lived near Mr Sowerberry's shop. His mother was a washerwoman and his father was a drunken soldier. He spent most of his time in the shop or in the streets. So this is how he gained his impudent temper and behaviour. Oliver had been living at the undertaker's shop for about a month. Mr Sowerberry found Oliver quite a hard-working and good-looking boy. He decided to teach Oliver all the mysteries of his trade. It was a cold winter, and the coffins were in great demand in the commercial phrase. Oliver gained a great deal of experience. Oliver accompanied his master to all funerals, in order to have strong nerves which were important for a professional undertaker. Shortly, Mr Sowerberry gave Oliver a black suit and a wooden stick, so as to look more serious at funerals. Noah tried to find faults with Oliver more often than before. His jealousy was increased by Oliver's promotion to the black suit and wooden stick. One day, Oliver and Noah had gone into the kitchen to have dinner. Mrs Charlotte was not in the kitchen at the time. Noah resolved to use that short period of time for aggravating young Oliver Twist. Noah pulled Oliver's hair and ears, calling him a 'sneak' and a 'fool.' He was very angry with Oliver.

"How is your mother, lazy boy?" said Noah to Oliver.

"She is dead. Don't say anything about her to me!" answered Oliver.

Oliver's face became red as he said this. He breathed quickly.

"And what did she die of?" asked Noah again.

"She died of broken heart. Somebody told me so. Don't say anything more!" cried Oliver.

"She was weak. And you are a weak boy, too!" said Noah.

"What did you say?" cried Oliver.

Oliver jumped to his feet with anger and seized Noah by the throat strongly. Then he shook him, gave a bow, and pushed him to the ground. Oliver was beyond himself with wrath. The cruel word to his dead mother had set his blood on fire. His eyes were bright and wild with anger. He was beating Noah with the power he had never known before.

"He will murder me!" cried Noah. "Mrs Charlotte! Help! Help! Oliver has gone mad! Mrs Charlotte!"

Noah's shouts were answered by a loud scream from Charlotte. She ran into the kitchen and seized Oliver tightly by his collar. Then she dragged Oliver into a dark cellar and locked him there. Noah told Mrs Sowerberry that Oliver started to beat him for no reason. He also did his best to cry bitterly with pain before Mrs Sowerberry. Mr Sowerberry was not at home at that moment. So she asked Noah to turn to Mr Bumble and tell him to come to her house directly. Noah ran out of the house at his fullest speed. Noah ran along the streets very quickly until he reached the workhouse-gate. He stopped near the gate for a minute to collect all his tears, and then entered the workhouse with a pretended horror on his face. As he entered the workhouse, he called for Mr Bumble as loudly as he could. Mr Bumble ran up to him at once.

"What? What happened?" asked Mr Bumble.

"Oliver has gone mad!" answered Noah. "He tried to murder me, and then he tried to murder Mrs Sowerberry. Oh, what a dangerous boy! Mrs Sowerberry asked you to come to her house directly, so as to calm Oliver down and punish him properly…"

"God!" said Mr Bumble. "I knew it! I had a strange presentiment that this dangerous boy would do something dreadful! Of course, I will go with you to Mrs Sowerberry. You are a good boy, Noah."

When Mr Bumble and Noah entered the house, Oliver was kicking at the cellar-door angrily. Mr Sowerberry had not yet returned home.

"Let me out! Let me out!" cried Oliver from the inside.

"Oliver, calm down at once!" cried Mr Bumble. "I am Mr Bumble. If you don't be calm, you will stay in this cellar until morning! Did you understand that?"

"Let me out!" cried Oliver, continuing to kick at the cellar-door.

"He is mad!" said Mrs Sowerberry.

"It is not madness, madam," said Mr Bumble. "It is meat. You have given him too much meat. You have raised a strong spirit in him. If you had given him only a plate of gruel, this would never have happened."

Mrs Sowerberry was very surprised at such unusual answer. She had given Oliver only some remains of meat which nobody else would eat.

"The only thing that you can do now is to leave him in the cellar for a few days. Then you must take him out and give him only gruel and a small piece of bread," said Mr Bumble indifferently.

When Mr Sowerberry returned home, Oliver's attack was explained to him in detail at once. The story was changed greatly, with many exaggerations in every sentence. Thus Oliver remained a prisoner in the cellar for a few days. Oliver cried bitterly in the cellar most of the time. A piece of bread was given to him two times a day as his daily meal. After two days, he was released from his imprisonment at last. Mr Sowerberry ordered him to go to his bed and stay there until morning. Oliver did as he was told straight away. It was a cold, dark evening. He lay motionless in his cold bed, planning the plan of his escape carefully. When the first ray of light appeared in the shutters, Oliver arose and opened the door softly. After one look around, he closed the door behind him and ran away quickly. He ran up to the hill which was a few miles away from the undertaker's shop. His heart beat quickly and he almost resolved to turn back. But then he thought the offence to his mother and continued to walk steadily. It was so early that nobody could see him walking away.

Oliver followed the main road without a stop. It was eight o'clock now. He was nearly five miles away from the town. Soon he sat down to rest by the side of the road, and began to think where he had better go and try to live. There was a sign on a big stone by which he was seated. This sign showed that it was seventy miles from that place to London. London! The place where nobody, even Mr Bumble, could ever find him! As this idea came to his mind, he jumped to his feet and began to walk again. By and by, he began to think of the means of getting there. He had a piece of bread, an old shirt, and two pairs of stockings. He had a penny in his pocket, too. Mr Sowerberry had given him this penny after one of the funerals as a gift. Oliver walked twenty miles that day, and all that time he ate nothing but a piece of bread and a cup of water which he asked from a kind woman on the road. When the night came, he found a hay-rick and slept there until morning. He was cold and hungry, and more lonely than he had ever felt before. Nevertheless, his tiredness made him fall asleep and forget his troubles quickly. He felt even more hungry when he got up the next morning. That day, he walked about twenty miles as well. His feet were sore, and his legs were so weak that they trembled beneath him. A few days passed in the same manner. When his bread was over, he begged of the kind people on the road. Very few people took any notice of him. But some people felt sorry for him and gave him one or two shilling to buy some crust of bread. On the seventh morning after his escape, Oliver limped slowly into the big city of London. The sun shone brightly. Many people passed him by in a hurry. None of them looked at him or helped him. He had no power to beg again. He sat down on a pavement to rest and think of what to do next in this huge city. He looked at the carriages and houses around him with curiosity. Suddenly, he saw a tall boy looking at him from the opposite side of the road. Then the boy crossed the road and walked close up to Oliver with a smile on his face.

"Hello? How do you do?" asked the boy.

The boy was about Oliver's own age. The boy had a common face, dark hair, and little eyes. His hat was too big for his little head. He wore a man's coat which reached nearly to his legs. He was, altogether, a confident and selfish young boy.

"I am very hungry and tired," answered Oliver. "I have walked a long way. I have been walking for seven days."

"Oh, I see. I have a small bread and a ham in my pocket. Take it, my poor friend," said the boy, taking out the bread from his pocket.

Oliver ate the bread and ham greedily in a moment. After that, he thanked the boy for being so kind to him.

"I live in London," said the boy. "I suppose you want a place to sleep tonight. I know a respectable old gentleman who is very kind to homeless children. I will introduce you to him. Would you like to go with me?"

"Yes, I did not sleep under a roof for a week," answered Oliver.

This unexpected offer of shelter was too good to be resisted. Oliver trusted his new friend without a doubt. Presently, his new friend introduced himself as Jack Dawkins. They walked through the streets for a long time. It was late afternoon when they reached an old house on a dirty street. He had never seen such dirty and poor street. The street was very narrow, and the air was full of nasty smells. Oliver thought of running away once again when they entered the old house. As Jack knocked at one of the doors, an ugly man looked out and told them to come in. The walls and ceiling were very dirty with age and dust. There was a big table before the fire, on which Oliver saw a candle, a bread and butter, and a plate. The ugly man was cooking some sausages in a frying-pan on the fire. His hair was red and his eyes were cunning. Jack called him Fagin friendly. There were five boys in the room. Jack introduced Oliver to Fagin and other boys joyfully. After that, he sat down on one of the beds in the room. Fagin looked at Oliver attentively and asked him to sit at the table. Soon he put a plate of sausage before Oliver and other boys. All the boys ate their supper gladly. Oliver ate his share and then fell asleep on one of the sacks in the corner of the room.

Chapter 3

Oliver Gets Into Trouble

It was late morning when Oliver awoke from a long sleep. There was nobody in the room but old Fagin. He was boiling some coffee for breakfast, whistling to himself as he stood by the fire. Oliver looked at Fagin with half-closed eyes. Fagin looked at Oliver and called him by his name. Oliver did not answer; he was still half-asleep. Fagin closed the door and took out some small box from a secret hole in the floor. Then he placed the box on the table and opened it carefully. The next moment he took from it a magnificent gold watch, sparkling with jewels. Oliver saw many rings, brooches, and bracelets in the box during his pretended sleep. By and by, Fagin put the watch back into the box and looked askew at Oliver. The boy's eyes were fixed on him sleepily. Fagin closed the box with a loud crash and jumped to his feet angrily, taking a knife in one hand.

"Are you awake? What did you see? Speak out!" said Fagin.

"I saw nothing, sir. I have just woken up," answered Oliver.

"Certainly, my dear boy," said Fagin with a calm voice.

Oliver got up and washed his face in a basin by the window. When he came up to the table, the box was gone. Just then Jack entered the room with a boy whom Oliver had seen the previous night. Jack introduced the boy to Oliver as Charles Bates. Soon they all sat down to breakfast and did not talk for a while.

"Well, I hope you have been at work this morning, my boys," said Fagin, looking at Jack seriously.

"Yes, we worked hard this morning. We got a couple of pocket-books," replied Jack.

Jack took out two pocket-books from his pocket and handed them to Fagin. Fagin looked at them carefully and smiled at the boys. After that, Charles Bates handed Fagin four silk handkerchiefs. They looked very pretty, indeed. Fagin was quite satisfied with the new findings.

"Well, you worked well this morning. I hope Oliver will learn to find handkerchiefs as easy as Charles Bates," said Fagin, looking at Oliver cunningly.

"If you teach me, I will learn how to find handkerchiefs as well," said Oliver.

As he said this, Charles Bates laughed loudly for a few minutes. The others began to laugh, too. Oliver could not understand the reason for their laughter. He could not also realize how the boys have found the pocket-books and handkerchiefs that morning. When the breakfast was over, the kind old gentleman and the boys played at a very curious game, which was performed in this way. Fagin put a small box in one pocket of his trousers and a note-case in the other. Then he walked up and down the room in imitation of the manner in which gentlemen walk about the streets every day. Sometimes he stopped at the fire-place, pretending to look at a shop-window. At such times, he looked carefully around him for fear of thieves in a very funny way. Oliver laughed till the tears ran down his face. All this time, the boys watched and followed Fagin very carefully. At last, Jack and Charles Bates came up to him unnoticeably and took from him quickly the small box and the note-case. When Fagin noticed that his box and the note-case were gone, he cried loudly for the police. At that moment the game was over. Soon Fagin put a handkerchief into his pocket, turned to Oliver and said:

"Try to take it out unnoticeably. Do this as you saw them do, when we were at play just a moment ago."

Oliver came up to Fagin silently, drew the handkerchief out of the pocket, and ran away quickly into the corner of the room.

"Did you do this?" asked Fagin.

"Yes. Here it is," said Oliver, showing it in his hand.

"You are a clever boy, Oliver," said Fagin. "I did not feel anything. Here is a shilling for you. You will be the greatest man of the time."

Oliver wondered how he could become the greatest man of the time by picking a handkerchief from the gentleman's pocket. But he trusted Fagin and did not ask what he meant by these words. For many days, Oliver remained in Fagin's house, taking part in the game already described or washing silk handkerchiefs (which were brought home in a great number every day). Oliver began to miss the fresh air and crowded streets outside. He wanted to work with other boys and be helpful for Fagin. At last, one morning, Fagin allowed Oliver to go out with other boys. Oliver went out of the house with Jack and Charles Bates gladly, wondering where they were going and what kind of job they would do. Shortly, they reached the open square in Clerkenwell. All of a sudden, Jack stopped, put his finger to his lips, and looked at his companions carefully.

"What is the matter?" asked Oliver.

"Do you see the old man at the book-stall?" asked Jack.

Penny each

"Yes, I see him," said Oliver.

"He will do," said Jack.

Oliver looked from one boy to the other in great surprise. But they did not explain him anything. The two boys walked slowly across the road and came up close to the old man. Oliver walked a few steps after them. The old gentleman looked very respectful and rich. He took a book from the stall and read it very attentively. Just then Oliver saw Jack take out a handkerchief from the gentleman's pocket! As Jack took out the handkerchief, he ran away with Charles Bates at full speed. At that moment Oliver understood the whole mystery of the handkerchiefs and the jewels in Fagin's box. He stood motionless for a while. Then he began to run away quickly, not knowing what he did and where he was running away. In the moment when Oliver began to run, the old gentleman put his hand in his pocket and noticed that his handkerchief was gone. As he saw Oliver running away so quickly, he naturally concluded him to be a thief. He cried loudly, 'Stop, thief!' And so the old gentleman and other citizens began to run after Oliver through the streets. 'Stop, thief! Stop, thief!' was heard from every corner of the street. The pursuit did not last long. After some time, a man stopped Oliver with a strong blow. The crowd soon gathered around him. Oliver lay on the ground, covered with dust and mud. An officer walked up to Oliver and asked seriously:

"Is this the boy, sir?"

"Yes," said the old gentleman.

"It wasn't me. Two other boys are the thieves. They are here somewhere," said Oliver.

"Oh, of course, you are not guilty. Stand up! We will find out everything soon," said the officer.

As Oliver stood up, the officer took him by the collar and dragged him along the streets. The old gentleman walked behind them as fast as he could. The crowd of people followed them to the police office with a loud, shameful cry. When they reached the police office, a tall man with black whiskers met them at the gate.

"What is the matter?" asked the man.

"A young thief," answered the officer.

"Go to the magistrate now," said the man indifferently.

The officer led Oliver to a stone cell and searched him carefully. Nothing was found in his pockets. Anyway, the officer locked him up in the cell and went away without a word. The old gentleman looked almost as sad as Oliver.

"There is something in that boy's face that touches my heart and interests me. Can he be innocent?" said the old gentleman to the officer.

The officer did not answer his question. He just told him to follow him to the magistrate at once. The magistrate was a thin, middle-sized man. His face was serious and red. The old gentleman bowed respectfully to the magistrate and sat down by his desk. The officer stood behind him.

"Who are you? What happened?" asked the magistrate.

"I am Mr Brownlow," answered the old gentleman. "I was robbed. Somebody stole a handkerchief from my pocket when I was standing at a book-stall."

"Are there any witnesses?" asked the magistrate.

"No," answered the officer.

"Bring the boy here," said the magistrate to the officer.

The officer brought Oliver to the magistrate's office straight away. Oliver was very scared. He tried to explain the whole story but his tongue failed him. He was very pale. The whole room seemed to turn round him.

"What is your name?" asked the magistrate.

Oliver did not answer the question. His body trembled from head to foot.

"I think he is ill. He will fall down now," said the old gentleman.

"Nonsense!" said the magistrate.

The next moment Oliver fainted to the floor. The magistrate and the officer looked at each other, but none of them tried to do something. Then the magistrate ordered the officer to carry Oliver to the cell and leave him there. The old gentleman stood up to his feet and said loudly:

"Stop! Don't take him away! He is innocent! Another boy committed the robbery. This boy had nothing in his pockets."

The magistrate was silent for a while.

"The boy is innocent. Clear the office then!" said the magistrate.

The officer took Oliver out of the police office and put him on the pavement. Oliver's face was deadly pale.

"Poor boy!" said the old gentleman to himself.

The old gentleman took a carriage on the road and laid Oliver carefully on the seat beside him.

Chapter 4

Oliver's Stay At Mr Brownlow's House

The carriage drove away quickly and stopped before a big house, in a quiet street near Pentonville. Mr Brownlow ordered his servant to prepare a bed for the young boy and deposit him there at once. Oliver was tended with great kindness and care in Mr Brownlow's house. But, for many days, he remained insensible and motionless. The sun rose and sank, and the boy lay still in his bed. He struggled with the heat of fever desperately. At last, one day, he awoke from a long dream. He was very weak and pale. He looked around anxiously and said:

"What room is this? Where am I?"

"Don't be scared," said the old lady. "You have been very ill. Lie down again."

Oliver placed his head on the pillow and fell asleep straight away. The old lady looked at him kindly and covered him with a blanket. Oliver's sleep was calm and peaceful. It was already a bright day when Oliver opened his eyes again. He felt cheerful and happy. The crisis of the fever passed safely. In three days, he was able to sit and walk as usual. The old lady was very glad about Oliver's recovery. She was always next to Oliver and became a good friend for him. Now, the old gentleman came in to take a good look at the recovered boy. Oliver was very pale from sickness. Nevertheless, he stood up and made a respectful bow to his benefactor.

"Poor boy! Do you feel better?" said Mr Brownlow, looking at Oliver pitifully.

"I feel better, sir. Thank you for your great goodness to me," said Oliver.

"What is your name, my dear boy?" asked Mr Brownlow.

"My name is Oliver Twist. I hope you are not angry with me," said Oliver.

"No, no," replied Mr Brownlow. "You have to rest. Don't be worried. You are safe and sound in my house."

Oliver felt really safe and sound in Mr Brownlow's house. His health was greatly improved and his fears were gone once and for all.

***

When the officer dragged Oliver to the police office, Jack and Charles Bates followed the crowd of people carefully. As Oliver and the officer entered the police office, they waited in the distance for a while and then ran away to the old house. They were very scared at that moment. They did not know how to explain Oliver's absence to Fagin. Anyway, they entered the old house as if nothing had happened. When Fagin saw that Oliver was not with them, he got up with an angry look.

"Where is Oliver?" he asked.

The young thieves looked uneasily at each other. But they made no reply.

"What happened to the boy? Speak out or I will beat you!" cried Fagin, coming closer to the scared boys.

Fagin looked so angry that Charles Bates decided to speak at last.

"Well, the officer has got him, and that's all," said Charles Bates.

Fagin stepped back in surprise. He looked even angrier than before. Just then he seized up the cup and prepared to hurl it at the boy's head, when a young gentleman entered the room.

"What is going on in here?" said the young gentleman. "Do you want to hurl this cup at me, Fagin? What happened?"

The gentleman who said these words was a tall man in a black coat. He had a brown hat on his head and a dirty handkerchief round his neck. A white dog entered the room and stood beside him. The gentleman kicked the dog in the leg and ordered it to go to the corner of the room. The dog obeyed its master at once.

"Why are you treating the boys so cruelly? I wonder why they don't murder you. I would if I was them," said the man.

"Well, Bill Sikes, you don't look joyful," said Fagin.

This was said in jest. Fagin explained his friend the reason for his anger in detail. Bill Sikes listened to him attentively without interruption.

"I am afraid that he may say something which will get us into trouble," said Fagin.

The man nodded in approval. There was a long pause. Every member of the respectable company seemed plunged in his own thoughts.

"Somebody must find out what has been done in the police office," said Sikes. "You, me, and the boys cannot go to the police office on any reason. We have to send somebody who will not draw police's attention."

How long they sat silently and looked at each other it is difficult to guess. Soon a young lady entered the room and greeted the two men joyfully.

"Of course! Nancy will go!" said Fagin loudly.

"Where?" asked the young lady.

"To the police office, my dear," answered Fagin. "You need only to find out what happened to the boy. Nobody about here knows anything about you."

The young lady agreed to go to the police office without much joy. She tied a clean apron over her gown and went out of the room. She walked through the streets carefully. By and by, she arrived at the police office in perfect safety. She entered by the back way and saw an old criminal in a big yard. Nancy stopped by the gate and asked the criminal to come up to her kindly.

"Is there a little boy here?" said Nancy. "He was taken here for robbery. He is my small, innocent brother. I am so worried about him."

"No," answered the criminal. "The robbery was committed by some other boy. The old gentleman has taken him in an insensible condition to his own house. His house is somewhere in Pentonville."

Nancy thanked the old man for his story and went away quickly. Soon she returned to the old house and told her friends everything she knew about Oliver.

"We must know where he is," said Fagin. "Charles Bates, go away and do not come back till you bring some news about him! Nancy, you must go with him as well. Bring Oliver here as soon as possible. Find him, that's all. I will know what to do next."

Charles Bates and Nancy went out of the room without another word. Fagin and Mr Sikes sat by the fire silently for a long time.

***

Oliver had a happy life at last. Everything was so quiet and everybody so kind to him that after the difficulties in which he had always lived it seemed like Heaven itself. Mr Brownlow bought some new clothes and shoes for him. Oliver felt very glad to think that there was no possible need to wear his old clothes again. One evening, Oliver entered Mr Brownlow's study to talk to him for a while. He greeted Mr Brownlow respectfully. He found himself in a little room full of different books and note-books. Mr Brownlow sat at his table, reading a book with a serious look. When he saw Oliver, he pushed the book away from him and told him to sit down. Oliver looked at the books in the study with great curiosity.

"There are many books here," said Mr Brownlow. "You will read them if you be a good boy. Now, listen to me attentively. I will talk to you seriously…"

"Oh, don't tell you are going to send me away, sir!" said Oliver sadly. "Let me stay here and be your servant. Don't send me back to the bad place I came from. Please!"

"My dear child, I will never send you away. You are a good boy. I know you have suffered great pain and sorrow. Please, tell me your story. I know that you are an orphan. Where did you come from? Who brought you up?"

Oliver started to tell his story in detail. He told Mr Brownlow of the orphan house and the workhouse, when a servant entered the study and announced Mr Grimwig. Mr Brownlow asked the servant to lead his friend into the study. Mr Brownlow turned to Oliver and said that Mr Grimwig was his old friend. Soon an old man entered the study, supporting himself with a thick stick. He was dressed in a blue coat and brown waistcoat. He smiled at Oliver and sat down at the table.

"Hello? Who are you?" said Mr Grimwig, looking at Oliver.

"This is Oliver Twist," said Mr Brownlow.

"How are you, boy?" asked Mr Grimwig.

"I feel much better, sir," answered Oliver.

At that moment Mr Brownlow asked Oliver to go downstairs and ask the servant whether the tea was ready or not. Oliver did as he was told at once.

"He is a good boy, isn't he?" asked Mr Brownlow.

"I don't know. Tell me his story first, and then I will tell you what kind of boy he is," replied Mr Grimwig.

And so Mr Brownlow told his friend the whole story about Oliver Twist from the beginning to the present moment. Mr Grimwig looked quite thoughtful and suspicious.

"He is a liar, my dear friend. He is deceiving you," said Mr Grimwig.

"He is not a liar! I swear," said Mr Brownlow.

Just then a servant entered the study with a hot tea and a cake on the trolley. He held a small parcel of books which Mr Brownlow ordered that morning. Suddenly, an interesting idea occurred to Mr Brownlow.

"My dear friend," said Mr Brownlow, "I know how to prove you that Oliver is a trustful boy. I ordered these books this morning without paying for them. I will give Oliver four pounds to pay for my books. He will pay for the books and come back at once. You will see."

Mr Brownlow asked the servant to call Oliver into the study. After a few minutes, Oliver stood before his benefactor and listened to him attentively. He was very glad to be useful for Mr Brownlow. He took four pounds and the books, and then went out of the room quickly.

"Do you really expect him to come back? He will join his old friends, the thieves, and never come back," said Mr Grimwig when Oliver left the study.

"He will come back," said Mr Brownlow.

As he said this, the two friends began to wait for Oliver silently. Mr Brownlow was completely sure that Oliver would come back soon. But his friend did not think so at all. Thus a few hours passed. It grew dark. The two old gentlemen continued to sit in silence, watching the clock on the table.

Chapter 5

Tells Of What Happened To Oliver After He Had Been Found By Nancy

Meantime, Oliver Twist was on his way to the book-stall. The book-stall was not very far from Mr Brownlow's house. Anyway, Oliver walked carefully so as not to get lost in the unknown streets. Oliver was very cheerful. He walked as quickly as he could, with the books under his arm. All of a sudden, a pair of arms grabbed him strongly into the empty corner of the street.

"Let me go! Who is it? What do you want from me?" cried Oliver.

The people on the street looked back in alarm.

"I found him at last!" said the young woman to the people. "He ran away from home a month ago and joined some thieves. Oh, I found him at last! I am his sister."

"I don't know her! She is not my sister! Help!" cried Oliver.

As Oliver cried loudly, the young women dragged him even stronger away from the street. Oliver was very frightened. But what could one poor child do! Nobody believed him in the street. Resistance was useless. In another moment, he was dragged farther into the dark street. After that, they stopped near an old house which Oliver had never seen before. Meanwhile, Fagin, Jack, and Sikes sat by the fire silently in the old house by which Oliver and Nancy stopped. Suddenly, Nancy entered the room, holding Oliver tightly by the hand.

"The boy is here at last! Look at him!" cried Fagin gladly.

The dog in the corner growled loudly. But soon it stopped to growl and lay down on the floor silently. Everybody received Oliver with a cry of laughter. Jack came up to him and made low bows to the scared boy respectfully. As he did so, he seemed to laugh even louder than before.

"Look at his new clothes," said Jack, touching Oliver's new jacket. "Look at his trousers and shoes! And his books, too!"

"I am glad to see you so well, Oliver," said Fagin. "Jack will give you another suit. This new suit looks too good for you. You can spoil it easily. Why didn't you write me you were coming to us today?"

At these words, Jack laughed at Oliver again and took the books and the five-pound note under his arm.

"What's that?" asked Fagin.

"That's mine!" cried Oliver angrily.

"No, no, my dear! That's mine. That's for our share of the trouble," said Fagin.

"The books and the five-pound note belong to the kind gentleman," said Oliver. "This gentleman took me into his house and nursed me when I was dying of the fever. Oh, please, send them back! Keep me here all my life long, but, please, send them back! He will think I stole them."

With these words, Oliver fell on his knees at the Fagin's feet.

"You're right, Oliver. He will think you stole them. Ha, ha, ha!" said Fagin.

At this moment Oliver ran to the door, trying to escape from the dangerous people. But his attempt of escape was in vain. Fagin dragged him by the collar and gave a strong blow on Oliver's shoulder with his club. He was raising the club for a second blow, when Nancy ran up to him and took it from his hand angrily. She threw it into the fire.

"You won't beat this boy again, Fagin!" cried Nancy.

Fagin lay down his club and dragged Oliver into the corner of the room. He did not want to provoke any fight in the house.

"You're a good friend for this boy," said Sikes.

"Yes, I am!" said Nancy. "I wish I had not brought him here. He is a thief from this night forth. Isn't that enough for the poor child?"

"Very kind words," said Fagin.

The girl said nothing more that night but sat silently by the fire with an angry look. Fagin led Oliver into a dark room and gave him an old suit.

"Take off the new suit and put on the old one. This new suit is mine now," said Fagin.

Oliver obeyed him unwillingly. Fagin rolled up the new suit under his arm and left the room, locking the door behind him with a derisive laughter. Oliver was very sad and tired. Soon he fell asleep on a cold bed in the dark room.

***

One early morning, Mr Bumble went out of the workhouse and walked steadily through the streets. His hat and coat seemed to shine in the morning sun. He held his cane very tightly in his hand. Mr Bumble always carried his head high, but this morning it was higher than usual. He looked very cheerful. Presently, he took a carriage to London. When he arrived in London, he went to a big inn and ordered a good breakfast for himself. Waiting for his breakfast, he drew his chair to the fire and opened the newspaper which lay on the table beside him. There was the following advertisement on the first page:

'FIVE GUINEAS REWAR'

'A young boy called Oliver Twist got lost on Thursday evening from his home at Pentonville, and has not been seen since then. The reward will be paid to any person who will find Oliver Twist, or give any information about him.'

And then followed a full description of Oliver's clothes and appearance, with Mr Brownlow's address at the end of the advertisement. Mr Bumble opened his eyes widely in surprise. He read the advertisement carefully for a few times. After five minutes, he was on his way to Pentonville. As he reached Mr Brownlow's house, he knocked at the door and explained the reason for his visit kindly. The old lady led him into the study straight away. Mr Brownlow and Mr Grimwig greeted the unexpected guest respectfully. Mr Bumble took his seat and looked at the gentlemen before him seriously. Then he put down his hat and unbuttoned his coat in a slow manner. The old lady stood by the door, waiting for the news about the lost boy.

"Do you know where Oliver Twist is now? What do you know of him?" asked Mr Brownlow.

Mr Bumble told the gentlemen of Oliver Twist and his life in the workhouse. He told them that Oliver had been an orphan with bad and treacherous qualities. He also told them of Oliver's attack on an innocent boy and his escape at night from his master's house. When Mr Bumble finished his story, Mr Brownlow stood up and began to walk to and fro for some minutes. At last, he stopped and said sadly:

"Mr Grimwig, you were right. Oliver was a liar."

"It can't be! I will never believe it! Oliver is a good boy!" said the old lady firmly.

"Silence!" said Mr Brownlow. "Never let me hear the boy's name again. Never! You may leave the room, Mr Bumble. Thank you for your true story."

Oliver was very distressed when he thought of his good friends. It was well for him that he could not know what they had said about him. Otherwise, it might have broken his heart once and for all.

***

About afternoon the next day, Fagin entered the room and told Oliver of his ingratitude and guilt, after so much trouble he had in the attempt of his discovery. Fagin also said about his help to Oliver, without which he might have died of hunger in the streets. Oliver's blood ran cold as he listened to Fagin's words. He understood the threats between his words clearly. He trembled with fear. Fagin patted Oliver on the head, saying that they would be very good friends if he devotes himself to robbery. Then he went out and locked the door behind him without a word. And so Oliver remained in the room for many days. He saw nobody but Nancy, who brought food and water for him two times a day. After two weeks, Fagin left the room without locking the door behind him. At last, Oliver could go out of the room and walk about the house freely. It was a very dirty place. The walls were dirty with dust and neglect. Spiders had built their webs in the corners of the walls and ceilings. Mice ran into their holes when Oliver walked from one room into the other. In all the rooms, the windows were closed. Oliver was very melancholy and scared. There was nothing he could do for his escape.

One afternoon, Jack commanded Oliver to clean his boots. He lit his pipe, swinging one leg to and fro disrespectfully. Oliver obeyed straight away, for fear of Fagin's wrath and punishment. When Oliver cleaned the boots, Jack looked at Oliver scornfully and said:

"Why don't you join our thief gang, Oliver? You can make your life much easier."

"I don't like it. I wish they would let me go. I want to leave this place," answered Oliver.

"Oh, it is impossible!" said Jack, laughing loudly for a while.

Oliver knew this very well. That is why he did not want to express his wishes more openly.

"Fagin will make you a thief anyway," said Jack. "You had better begin at once. You are only losing your time now, Oliver. Just take pocket-handkerchiefs and watches, and Fagin will be satisfied. That's very simple, you know."

"Certainly! That's very simple," said Fagin, entering the room suddenly.

The conversation did not continue anymore because Fagin was accompanied by a lady and a gentleman who Oliver

had never seen before. As they spoke to each other, Oliver understood that the lady's name was Miss Betsy and the gentleman's Mr Chitling. Shortly, Fagin sent Jack on an errand and sat by the fire with his friends. They talked about their hard trade and good proficiency. Fagin praised highly Jack and Charles Bates, telling of their cunning and tricky qualities. At last, the conversation finished and Fagin's friends left the room. From this day, Oliver was not left alone. He played the same old game with handkerchiefs every day with Fagin and other boys. At other times, Fagin told them stories of robberies he had committed in his youth. In short, Fagin tried to change Oliver's mind and thoughts. He wanted Oliver to join his gang as soon as possible.

Chapter 6

A Dangerous Plan

It was a cold, windy night. Fagin came out of his house, buttoning his long coat around his body. He paused for a moment and then walked down the street quickly. The house to which Oliver was dragged was in the neighbourhood of Whitechapel. He walked fast, looking around carefully at times. The mud lay thick on the stones and a white mist hung over the streets. It was raining. He continued to walk through many wide and narrow streets carefully. Finally, he stopped near an old house and knocked at the door softly. After exchanging a few words with a person, he entered the house and walked upstairs quickly. Sikes greeted Fagin joyfully and asked him to sit down by the fire. A dog growled in the corner of the room as usual. But then it wagged its tail to show that everything was fine. Nancy came in and greeted Fagin in a friendly manner. Then she put a bottle of wine on a table and filled the glass cheerfully. The two men took the glasses and drank its contents gladly. Fagin looked at his companions seriously.

"Well, and now about the house at Chertsey," said Fagin. "When will we do that? Such a wonderful house for robbery!"

"We cannot do that," said Sikes. "One my friend was hanging about the place for two weeks. The dwellers are at home all the time. It is a useless business, Fagin."

Fagin looked disappointed at this information. He was very thoughtful for some time. Then came a long silence. Sikes watched him attentively from time to time. Nancy sat in her chair, looking at the fire sadly.

"Fagin, I was there last night," said Sikes. "The windows were closed as tightly as a jail. A man cannot enter the house through the window. But there is one small window we can break. All we need is a small boy who would creep in and rob the house at night silently."

"A boy!" said Fagin.

Nancy looked at him suspiciously.

"Oliver is the very boy for our business!" said Fagin. "He has been in good training last two weeks. He suits for this robbery very well, as the other boys are all too big. He will do everything we want, Sikes."

"Well, he is just of the size I want," said Sikes.

"When are you going to do that?" asked Fagin.

"The night after tomorrow," answered Sikes.

"Good," said Fagin. "Nancy can bring the boy here tomorrow night. Now we must hold our tongues and keep quiet."

Nancy nodded in approval. After some discussion, it was decided that Nancy must come to Sikes's house the next evening and bring Oliver away with her. When everything was arranged, Sikes took out a box of housebreaking tools and opened it before his companions. Fagin and Nancy were satisfied with its contents very much. And so everything was arranged for the robbery of the big house at Chertsey. By and by, Fagin said good-night to his companions and left the house joyfully. He walked his way through the mud to the old house where he lived. When he entered the house, he went upstairs silently. It was too late for a conversation with Oliver. The boy was sleeping in his bed. His face was sad and pale.

“Not now. Tomorrow,” said Fagin to himself, leaving the room.

When Oliver woke up in the morning, he saw a ready breakfast on the table before the fire. Fagin greeted him more cheerfully than usual.

“This night you will be taken to the house of Bill Sikes, Oliver,” said Fagin. “You will stay there only for one night. Don’t be scared. You will come back to us again. We will never send you away. No, no!”

Oliver’s face became pale with fear. He was afraid of asking the reason of his departure this night. He knew that he had no other choice but to obey Fagin’s order. Fagin left Oliver in the late afternoon, leaving a book for him to read. He burnt a candle and asked Oliver to wait for Nancy in the evening. When the old man left the house, Oliver began to think of the words he had said. He was sure that he was chosen to commit some robbery or something similar to that. After one hour, a loud knock at the door alarmed him.

“Who is here?” asked Oliver with trembling voice.

“Me. Only me. Nancy,” said the voice behind the door.

Oliver opened the door at once. He saw that she was very pale and worried. The girl sat down by the fire rapidly, shivering with cold for a moment.

“Now, Oliver, are you ready?” said Nancy. “I have come from Bill Sikes. You must go with me. Don’t be scared.”

Oliver knew that it was hopeless for him to beg for mercy. He said that he was ready. Nancy watched him attentively for a while.

“Oh, poor boy!” said Nancy. “I can’t help you. I tried to change their mind, but all in vain. I have saved you from beating once, but now I can do nothing. They have some job for you this night. Be calm and quiet. Remember this! Just do what they will order you to do!”

As she said this, she told Oliver to put on his coat and follow her without a word. There was a carriage waiting for them on the road. When they took their seat, the carriage moved away at once. The driver did not want any direction. He knew where to drive very well, as it seemed. Nancy held Oliver tightly by the hand. All was so quick, that he had no time to understand where he was, or how he came there. Shortly, the carriage stopped at the house to which Fagin had gone on the previous evening. Oliver wanted to cry for help desperately. But the fear inside of him seemed to make his tongue numb forever. While he hesitated, he was already in the house and the door was closed behind him. Sikes met them at the entrance door with a joyful smile.

“He is here, Bill,” said Nancy.

“I am glad to see him here,” said Sikes. “Come here, young boy. Let me read you a lecture which you must keep in mind now.”

Bill Sikes took Oliver by the hand and stood the boy in front of him.

“Do you know what it is?” asked Sikes, taking a small pistol out of his pocket.

“Yes, sir,” replied Oliver.

“It is loaded,” continued Sikes. “Well, when you speak a word when you are outside with me, except when I speak to you, one of the bullets will be in your head immediately. Did you understand me?"

Oliver nodded in approval. After that, Nancy set the table for dinner quickly and asked them to sit at the table. Oliver had no great appetite at that moment. His hands shook with fear all the time. When the dinner was finished, Oliver sat down by the fire without a word. A few hours passed in the same manner. Oliver was waiting impatiently for the fearful command from the thieves. At last, Sikes got up and looked at Oliver seriously.

"The time has come!" said Sikes.

Nancy gave a long coat to Oliver and told him to be careful. Sikes took Oliver by the hand firmly and led him out of the room. Oliver turned for a moment in the hope of meeting a look from Nancy. But she sat in front of the fire and did not care about Oliver at all. It was a cold night when they got into the street. The clouds looked black and stormy. The road was covered with filth and mud. Nobody seemed to move in that part of the town. The windows of the houses were all closed, and the streets through which they passed were silent and empty. Thus they walked through many streets for a long time. Oliver had no idea where they were going and what he must do for the thieves. They walked quickly till they had passed Hyde Park and were on their way to Kensington. When they reached Kensington, Sikes took a carriage and said the driver silently where to go. As they passed many miles, Oliver wondered where Sikes meant to take him. At last, they stopped near a small inn called the 'Coach and Horses.' And there they dismounted and began to walk rapidly. They passed many rich houses on both sides of the way. The night was very dark. A damp mist spread itself over the dark street. It was very cold, too. The leaves on the trees moved noiselessly in the night wind. Not a word was spoken between Sikes and Oliver. They still continued to walk in the dark streets. Presently, they reached a lonely house. The house was very decayed and ruinous. No light was visible inside of the house. The house was dark. Sikes and Oliver knocked at the door softly and came in.

"Hello!" said a voice, as soon as they entered the house.

"Hello, Toby Crackit. We are here at last," said Sikes.

Sikes pushed Oliver before him and they entered a dark room with a smoky fire. There were three broken chairs, a bed, and a table in the room. Toby Crackit had very usual appearance: red hair, small nose, blue eyes, and thin body.

"Who is it?" asked Toby, pointing at Oliver.

"The boy. Only the boy who will do our business tonight," answered Sikes.

"Good," said Toby. "Now sit down by the fire and rest for a while. Because you will go out with me tonight."

Oliver looked at Sikes in silent wonder. He sat by the fire, without knowing where he was or what was happening around him. Soon Toby Crackit gave them some food and water, and sat beside them silently. Sikes ate his food very greedily. Oliver could eat nothing but a small crust of bread. He was so tired and worried that he fell asleep by the warm fire for some time. After an hour or so, he was awakened by Toby Crackit who was saying that it was half-past one. In a moment, Sikes jumped to his feet and was busy with some preparation. They wrapped their heads with dark shawls and put on their long black coats. After that, they put several pistols into their pockets. Sikes took some housebreaking tools as well. Toby went to the door and returned, saying that all was quiet. The two robbers went out of the house with Oliver between them. It was now very dark. The fog was much heavier than it had been a few hours ago. The air was very damp. They crossed a small bridge near the house and began to walk forward without a word. Soon they arrived in Chertsey. They walked quickly through the main street of the town, which at that hour was fully empty. There was nobody in the street. After a few miles, they stopped before a lonely house surrounded by a wall. They climbed the wall one by one in a moment. Before Oliver had time to look around, Sikes told him to lie on the grass beside them. Oliver did so at once. After that, they walked carefully towards the house. And now Oliver realized everything in a second. They were going to rob the house! And he must help the thieves, or they would kill him without mercy! Oliver fell on his knees and began to beg to let him go. Sikes did not mind his appeals at all. He took out his pistol and dragged the scary boy to the house.

"Silence!" whispered Sikes. "Say another word and I will kill you here straight away. Do what I say to you and you will stay alive!"

As he said this, they went to the house and stopped by a small window above the ground. The window was so small that no adult could get through it. But it was large enough for a boy of Oliver's size. Sikes broke the window with one of his tools without much noise. It stood wide open now.

"Now listen, you stupid boy," whispered Sikes, "I am going to put you through this window. Take this small lantern with you and go silently upstairs to the street door. Open this door and let us in. And keep quiet all the time!"

Oliver nodded in fear. The next moment Sikes put Oliver softly through the window and then placed him on the floor inside. Oliver took the lantern with shaking hand and looked around carefully. Then he walked upstairs as noiselessly as he could.

"What's that?" said Toby, looking around attentively.

"Nothing," said Sikes.

Oliver was walking upstairs with the lantern in his hand. All of a sudden, there was a cry in the house. Oliver did not know what to do next. The cry repeated once again. Then a light appeared in the house. He saw two men at the top of the stairs and then he heard a loud noise. After that, he fell down on the floor without understanding what had happened to him. But the next moment all was clear – he was shot by one of the men and lay on the floor, bleeding and breathing hard. Sikes fired a few times at the men, crying to Oliver to run away. But it was too late. Oliver lay unconscious on the floor. Sikes told Toby Crackit to run away right away. And so they ran away into the darkness without Oliver. A cold feeling crept into the boy's heart, and he saw or heard no more.

Chapter 7

A Short Subject That May Be Important In This Story

The things were happening in the workhouse. The room was very quiet. A sick woman lay there. Her body was bent by age and her face was pale and wrinkled. It was a small room. A white candle was burning on the table. There was another old woman, watching by the bed. A young gentleman stood by the fire silently.

"It is a cold night, Mrs Corney," said the young gentleman.

"Very cold, sir," replied Mrs Corney.

The conversation was interrupted by the cry from the sick woman.

"Oh! She cries again," said the young gentleman.

"If she lives a couple of hours, I will be surprised," said Mrs Corney. "She will die tonight. But now she is sleeping for the last time."

The young gentleman bent over the bed and nodded in agreement. Then he resumed his place by the warm fire again. Mrs Corney wrapped herself in her shawl and sat at the foot of the bed. They sat in silence for some time.

"Did she say anything more today?" asked the young gentleman.

"Not a word," replied Mrs Corney. "She rose from the pillow for a while and soon dropped off. She has no power in her. She will die for sure…"

Just then the sick woman raised upright and stretched her arms towards her.

"Who's that?" asked the sick woman, looking at the young gentleman by the fire.

"Silence! Lie down, lie down!" said Mrs Corney.

"I will never lie down again alive! Let me tell you something," said the sick women.

She took Mrs Corney by the hand and pushed her to the bedside. She was about to speak, when she looked at the young gentleman again.

"He must go away! I will speak to you face to face," said the sick woman.

Mrs Corney asked the young gentleman to go out of the room. The latter did so unwillingly. When they were alone, the sick woman turned to Mrs Corney and said:

"Now listen to me. I once nursed a pretty young woman. I found her alone in the street. Her feet were cut and bruised with long walking. She gave birth to a boy and then died. Well… I robbed this dead woman. I stole something…"

"Stole what?" asked Mrs Corney.

"The only thing she had," replied the sick woman. "She had kept it always in her bosom. It was a gold locket. Real gold! She trusted me. But I stole it! This locket would change the child's life for better. Poor girl! She was so young…"

"What is the boy's name?" asked Mrs Corney.

"They called him Oliver. The gold I stole is in…"

The sick woman dropped dead on the pillow. Mrs Corney bent over the woman to hear the reply. But it was too late. The woman lay dead in her bed. The next moment Mrs Corney saw something in her hand. She opened her hand and saw a beautiful gold locket. She took it and went out of the room carelessly.

Chapter 8

Mr Fagin And His Company

When the sick woman died in the workhouse, Mr Fagin sat in his old house – the same from which Oliver had been taken by Nancy. He looked at the fire thoughtfully for a long time. At the table behind him sat Jack, Charles Bates, and Mr Chitling. Mr Fagin wore his hat because it was quite a cold night. He had a small pipe between his teeth, which he removed for a while to fill it with new tobacco. There was a long silence in the room. Suddenly, there was a loud knock at the door. Everybody in the room looked alarmed and worried. Fagin turned to Charles Bates and told him to open the door. Charles Bates obeyed at once. He took a candle in his hand and came up to the door carefully. As he opened the door, he saw a dark figure with a shawl which had concealed the lower part of the face. The figure opened his face and Charles Bates recognized his friend Toby Crackit.

"How are you, Toby?" asked Charles Bates.

Toby Crackit did not answer his question. He entered the room, drew a chair to the fire, and looked at Fagin seriously. Toby looked very scared and confused. He did not know how to open a conversation for some time. Fagin watched him attentively, trying to understand what had happened to him. But in vain. Toby looked tired and dirty. Something bad had happened to him for sure.

"First, I want to ask you something… How is Bill Sikes?" said Toby.

"What? He was not with you?" asked Fagin in surprise.

"Didn't he come here before me? You don't mean to say that…" said Toby.

"Where are they?" asked Fagin. "Sikes and the boy? Where are they hiding? Why did they not come here with you?"

"The robbery failed," answered Toby. "They fired and hit the boy. We ran away with Sikes into the fields. We ran away in different direction in order to confuse the men who were following us. The boy remained in the house, bleeding on the floor. The whole town was awake and the men and dogs chased us in the fields!"

"The boy!" cried Fagin.

"We wanted to take him with us," said Toby. "But it was too late. We had to run away at once. The boy was shot. He lay motionless on the floor. I think he was dead, but I am not sure. That's all I know about him."

Fagin screamed loudly with anger and then went out of the house into the dark street. He walked along the street in a wild manner for a few minutes. Then he became calmer and began to breathe more freely. He continued to walk quickly without a stop. Soon he reached a street with many different shops and inns. He was well known in this place, as many men nodded when he passed along. He greeted them in the same way. By and by, he stopped by the old inn and entered it, looking anxiously about all the time. He asked some men inside whether they saw Bill Sikes that night or not. Nobody saw Sikes that night. Fagin was very disappointed. The fear grew stronger within him with every minute. Fagin left the inn and took a carriage to Sikes's house. As he reached the house, he came in without a knock at the door and ran upstairs quickly. Nancy was alone, lying with her head on the table. Fagin closed the door behind him and looked at Nancy anxiously. She raised her head slowly. She looked very distressed and scared. She did not say a word. There was a short pause for a moment. During the silence, Fagin looked about the room to make sure there was no Sikes there. Sikes was not there. He tried to open a conversation twice or trice, but the girl did not pay any attention to him. At last, he tried one more time.

"Where is Bill Sikes now, Nancy?" asked Fagin.

The girl did not answer him. She began to cry bitterly.

"And the boy!" said Fagin. "Poor little child! They left him alone in a ditch of blood! Only think of it, Nancy!"

"The child is better where he is now, than among us," said Nancy. "I hope he is dead now. The worst is over for him now."

"What?" said Fagin in surprise.

Fagin was surprised to hear such cruel words from Nancy. He did not know what to say at that moment. That is why he just sat down at the table and looked at his companion silently. Nancy turned her face away from him in disgust.

"I say it again," said Nancy suddenly, "I hope the boy is dead now and away from you and Sikes. I am sure Bill is safe somewhere. Just wait for him for a few days. He will come back."

Fagin was quite satisfied with such words. He had nothing more to say. He stood up and left the room without saying good-bye to Nancy. He was on his way home, leaving his young companion asleep on the table. It was midnight. The weather was dark and cold. He reached the corner of his own street, when a dark figure ran after him quickly.

“Fagin!” cried a voice behind him. “It is me. I have been waiting for you here for two hours. Where have you been?”

“Ah! It is you!” said Fagin. “I was away on some business tonight, and nothing good came out of it.”

The stranger did not say a word. He just entered Fagin’s house and asked him to close the door softly. Fagin closed the door behind him and led the man into the parlour. Toby Crackit slept in the back room below, and the boys were asleep in the front one. As Fagin entered the parlour, he lit the candle and asked the stranger to sit down by the warm fire. They talked for some time in whispers. Then their conversation became loud and Monks, by which name Fagin called the strange man, got up and said angrily:

“I tell you again, it was not planned well! The boy wasn’t ready to commit the robbery!” said Monks.

“I saw it wasn’t easy to train him,” said Fagin. “He was not like other boys. If he is alive, we will find him and make him a thief. But if he is dead…”

“If he is dead, it is not our fault!” said Monks.

With these words, their conversation finished and they did not talk anymore. It was an early morning. They were so tired that they fell asleep by the warm fire straight away.

Chapter 9

Oliver's New And Kind Friends

That night, when the robbery failed, Bill Sikes and Toby Crackit were running away from their chasers in the fields. Two servants of the house, Mr Giles and Mr Brittles were running after them with guns in their hands. But the two men had not caught up with the robbers. The robbers were already too far to be found. That is why the two men decided to return home empty-handed. The air was very cold. The mist rolled along the ground like a dense cloud of smoke. The grass was wet. When they came home, Oliver still lay motionless on the floor. But soon he began to come to his senses slowly. As he heard the two men enter the house, he cried with pain and fear in a low voice. Firstly, Mr Giles and Mr Brittles did not move. But then they recalled the robber they had hit down the stairs. They were scared for a while. They looked at each other in perplexity. After some time, they took a dog in front of them and went downstairs carefully. When the two men went downstairs, they saw Oliver Twist, lying speechless and motionless on the floor.

"A boy!" cried Mr Giles in surprise.

"One of the thieves!" said Mr Brittles.

They took the boy by the arm (fortunately not by the injured arm) and placed him into the hall on the floor. As they did so, Mr Brittles ran to the top of the house to tell the lady of the house and her niece what had happened to them. He reached the room at the top of the house in less than two minutes.

"Here he is!" cried Mr Brittles. "One of the thieves! I shot him, and Giles helped me to run after the other thieves.

Unfortunately, we could not catch up with the robbers. But one of them is lying injured in the hall below."

The two ladies ran downstairs to see the injured robber. They were very surprised to see an injured boy on the floor. One of the ladies told Mr Giles to saddle the horse and drive to Chertsey immediately. Mr Giles was to bring a doctor as fast as possible. When Mr Giles went out of the house, Mr Brittles carried Oliver to one of the bedrooms upstairs carefully. Meanwhile, the two ladies sat silently in a parlour. One of the ladies was old and serious, and the other young and worried. They were waiting for Mr Giles and the doctor impatiently. At last, after one hour, Mr Giles and the doctor entered the house and went upstairs to see the injured robber. The doctor seemed troubled by the fact of the robbery committed by such a young boy. Anyway, he agreed to examine the injured boy. The doctor was absent for an hour or so. Then he asked the ladies to bring him some clean cloth and clothes for the boy. There was a small commotion in the house. The two ladies ran up and down the stairs quickly. Finally, the doctor returned and sat beside the two ladies in the parlour. He looked tired and anxious.

"It is a very unusual thing, Mrs Maylie," said the doctor, looking at the old lady.

"He is not in danger, I hope?" asked Mrs Maylie.

"I think he will be fine. Do you know anything about the robber?" said the doctor.

"No," replied Mrs Maylie.

"The boy doesn't look dangerous," said the doctor. "On the contrary, he seems to be a very kind boy. You can visit him now."

The doctor told the two ladies to follow him into the bedroom where his patient lay. The robber was just a young boy. His wounded arm was bound and crossed on his breast. His head lay motionlessly on the pillow. The doctor looked at his patient in silence. The old lady sat in a chair by the bedside and gathered Oliver's hair from his face. As she leaned over him, her tears fell on his forehead. The boy moved and smiled in his sleep.

"This child cannot be the pupil of the robbers!" said the young lady.

"Miss Rose," said the doctor to the young lady, "crime like death is not limited to young and old age. The youngest are mostly the victims of it."

"Oh, how young he is!" said Mrs Rose. "He never has known a mother's love or the comfort of a home. Hunger and cold have forced him to work with robbers. My dear aunt, we cannot drag this sick child to a prison!"

"My dear Rose, I would never harm such a young child!" said Mrs Maylie.

"Well, we must talk to the boy as soon as possible," said the doctor. "We must ask him about his life. He will wake up in an hour or so. Soon we will understand whether he is a good or bad boy."

The two ladies nodded in agreement. But Oliver did not wake up after one hour. Many hours passed, and still Oliver slept heavily. It was late afternoon when the doctor said that the boy was awaken at last. The boy was very ill and weak from the loss of blood. The conversation was very long. Oliver told them all his story with a voice of the sick child. When he finished his story, he fell asleep once again. The two ladies and the doctor went to the parlour in order to decide what to do next. Mr Giles and Mr Brittles were there as well.

"How is the boy? If he is dead, I can go to prison," said Mr Giles.

"Quite well, Mr Giles," answered the doctor. "He did not die. You don't need to be afraid. The robber is a young boy. We heard his story just a moment ago. He is just an innocent boy with a hard life. I think there is no need for calling the police."

"Oh!" said Mr Brittles, "I sent for officers this morning. They may be here at any moment!"

The doctor looked very disappointed to hear that. He wanted to save the boy from the prison, but now all his attempts were in vain. Presently, the officers from Chertsey came in and greeted the dwellers of the house respectfully. Then one of the officers turned to the doctor and said:

"Mr Losberne, tell us about the robbery? How has it happened?"

Mr Losberne told the whole story in detail. Then Mr Giles and Mr Brittles told the officers about their long chase after the robbers.

"So this is all about the robbery, isn't it? Didn't you see any of the robbers?" asked one of the officers.

"No," asked Mr Giles.

"We couldn't catch up with any of the robbers, sir," said Mr Brittles.

"Well, what about this boy that the servants were talking about?" said the officer.

"Nothing at all," said Mr Giles. "Just one of the frightened servants was too unlucky yesterday and was shot by the robber into his arm. The boy has nothing to do with the robbery."

"What he says is right," said Dr Losberne. "The boy is innocent. He is a servant in this house. I think we can see the place where the thieves tried to enter the house."

Thus the doctor led the officers to the small window through which Oliver Twist entered the house. Dr Losberne walked very anxiously. He showed the officers the window and went back to the parlour. The two ladies looked very worried. They wanted to save the poor boy from prison very much. Dr Losberne, Mr Giles, and Mr Brittles sat in the parlour without saying a word. By and by, the officers come back to the parlour and looked at the dwellers seriously.

"We checked the window carefully," said one of the officers. "No doubt, the robbers tried to enter the house through the small window. Now, if you please, we would like to see the boy upstairs."

Dr Losberne led the officers into the bedroom silently. The officers looked at the boy attentively for a few minutes. Then they went out of the room. They did not trouble themselves very much about Oliver. Finally, the officers left the house and went to Chertsey, promising to find the robbers as soon as possible. The next morning, there came rumours that two robbers were at Kingstone. But then the rumours were forgotten once and for all, as it seemed. Meanwhile, Oliver slowly recovered himself under the care of Mrs Maylie, Mrs Rose, and Dr Losberne. The poor child brought them great peace and happiness. After two weeks, Oliver got better and could talk to his benefactors usually. He hoped that when he grew strong again, he could

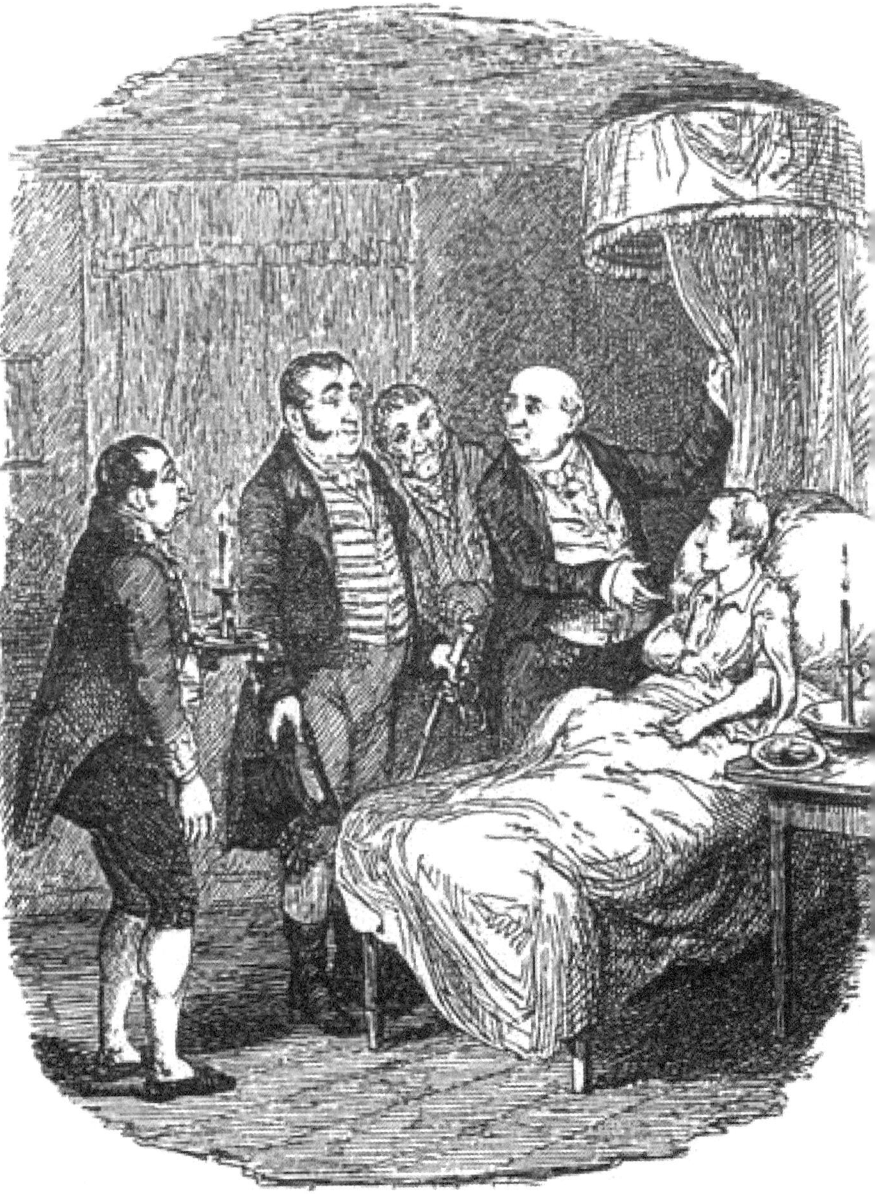

do something to show his gratitude to them. He wanted to do something that would prove to them that their kindness had not been in vain.

"Poor boy!" said Rose, when Oliver thanked her for her kindness. "You will have many opportunities of showing us your gratitude. But now just lie in your bed and rest well."

"You're right, madam. I was only thinking that I am ungrateful now," said Oliver.

One day, when Oliver was fully recovered, he told Dr Losberne about Mr Brownlow and the kind old lady who had nursed him during his fever. Dr Losberne was very curious to meet Mr Brownlow and hear his story about Oliver. That is why he asked Oliver to show him the house in which Mr Brownlow lived. Oliver was very glad to hear that. And so they took a carriage to London at once. As Oliver knew the name of the street, they reached the house soon afterwards. When the carriage turned into the street, Oliver's heart beat very fast with joy. The carriage stopped near a big, white house. Dr Losberne knocked at the door softly. Unfortunately, nobody opened the door. The white house was empty and there was a sign in the window 'For Sale.' Oliver was very sad and disappointed. Dr Losberne went to the neighbouring house and asked what happened to Mr Brownlow. The answer was quite surprising: Mr Brownlow sold his house and then went to West Indies two months ago. Oliver could hardly believe that. They returned home without saying a word in a carriage.

This occasion did not change the attitude of his benefactors towards Oliver. He grew healthier with every day. Finally, his life became peaceful and safe. It was a very lovely spring. One day, Mrs Maylie took Oliver and Rose to her summer house for a small holiday. Mr Giles and Mr Brittles remained in her usual house in order to look after it when their mistress was absent. In the summer house, Oliver ran about the fields gladly all day long. He spent his day in gathering flowers and lying in the haystack by the house. It was a very happy time for him. The days were peaceful and the nights brought him neither fear nor danger. He began to read the books one by one. He listened with pleasure to all they said to him about his education. So three month passed quickly. Spring flew swiftly by, and summer came. Still, the same calm life went on at the house, and the same cheerful atmosphere lasted among its dwellers. Oliver was as healthy and happy as he had never been before in his life.

Chapter 10

There Is A Sudden Change In Oliver's Happiness

One beautiful afternoon, Mrs Maylie and Oliver came back home after a long walk. Rose did not accompany them because of her unwellness. She was waiting for them in the parlour when Oliver and Mrs Maylie came home. The old lady seemed tired and worried. She sat down to the piano and began to play sadly. After playing for a few minutes, she stopped playing the piano. Oliver realized that she was crying.

"Rose, I am so worried about you," said Mrs Maylie, turning to Rose. "What I will do without you? You must recover as soon as possible. I never saw you so ill…"

"I have tried very hard, but I cannot help this. I fear I am very ill," said Rose.

Rose was sick, indeed. Her face changed to a white marble. Its expression had not lost its beauty, but it was changed. Oliver, who watched Rose attentively, noticed that she was distressed and weak. Nevertheless, Rose assured them she would be better soon. But Mrs Maylie was very afraid of losing Rose who has so long been her happiness. The day passed with a sad atmosphere in the house. When morning came, Mrs Maylie's worst fears come true. Rose was in the first stage of a dangerous fever.

"You must be fast, Oliver," said Mrs Maylie. "This letter must be sent to Dr Losberne at once. You must carry it to Chertsey immediately. Then the people at the inn will send it by the post carriage. You can do it, I know."

Oliver nodded in agreement.

"Here is another letter," said Mrs Maylie, showing Oliver another envelope. "This one is for my son Harry Maylie. Did you understand?"

With these words, she gave Oliver the letters and told him to go to Chertsey without delay. Oliver quickly ran across the fields to Chertsey. He did not stop even for a few seconds to recover his breath, until he came to the inn on the marketplace. Here he stopped and looked around attentively. Presently, he found the landlord of the inn and explained him the whole situation. The landlord took the letters and asked a man to saddle a horse and deliver the letters to the post office. Oliver was very excited and desperate. At last, the letters were sent quickly. Oliver went out of the inn with a lighter heart. He was walking to the gate, when he accidentally stumbled against a tall man dressed in a black coat.

"I beg your pardon, sir. I did not see you," said Oliver.

"You! What are you doing here?" asked the man.

The man shook his feast as he said these words angrily. He was very nervous. Oliver looked for a moment at the madman and then ran away as fast as he could. Soon he reached home and told Mrs Maylie that the letters had been sent successfully. Rose was getting worse rapidly. Dr Losberne arrived within an hour. He examined the poor girl carefully and said that her disease was quite dangerous. That day, Oliver could not sleep well. He thought of Rose and her disease all the time. His helplessness tortured him greatly. Morning came, and the house was lonely and still. People spoke only in whispers. Oliver gathered some flowers for Rose from the garden by the house. The day passed in tears and prayers. Another morning. The sun shone brightly, but nobody in the house was as happy as before. Oliver thought of the kindness he had received from the young lady during his stay in the house. They sat in the parlour silently. Rose was sleeping deeply at that moment. She would wake up soon, either to recover or say good-bye and die. By and by, Dr Losberne entered the parlour and looked at Mrs Maylie and Oliver anxiously.

"We all must be calm," said Dr Losberne.

"How is Rose? Oh, she is dead!" cried Mrs Maylie.

"No! She will live for years to come," said the doctor.

The old lady cried with happiness for a long time. Oliver cried with happiness as well. He was very glad to hear such good news. The next morning, he went to the field to gather some fresh flowers for Rose. As he walked along the road, a carriage stopped beside him. A man in a black hat told Oliver to come up to him kindly. Oliver recognized Mr Giles immediately.

"How is Mrs Rose? Better or worse?" asked Mr Giles.

"Much better! Dr Losberne says that all danger is over now," answered Oliver.

Mr Giles did not say another word. He took Oliver by the hand and led him inside. There was another gentleman in the carriage. He introduced himself as Harry Maylie. Thus they were on their way to Mrs Maylie's house. Oliver watched the new comer with curiosity. He was about thirty years old and of the middle height. His face was kind and frank. When they reached the house, Mrs Maylie was waiting for her son by the gate. They greeted each other very emotionally.

“Mother, how is Rose now?” said Harry. “Is she better? I was so worried about her these two days. I came as fast as I could. You know how much Rose means for me…”

“Rose is better, Harry. She knows you are here,” said Mrs Maylie.

As they talked at the gate, Dr Losberne went out of the house to greet Harry Maylie. The doctor told him the whole story about his patient’s situation, which was quite well and stable. That day passed in a happy atmosphere. Oliver woke up the next morning with a joyful smile on his face. All the troubles have already passed, and Rose and her family were as glad as before. Oliver began his occupations with more pleasure than he had known for many days. The birds on the trees and flowers in the field appeared more beautiful to him than one week ago. The melancholy was gone very quickly, as if by magic. Oliver brought to home many fresh flowers as usual. The flowers were given to Rose immediately, as she liked to feel their fragrance in her room. That day, Oliver sat in the room at the back of the house, reading one of the books from the library. It was already twilight. Oliver felt a little sleepy at that moment. Oliver knew that he was in the little room, and that his books were lying on the table before him. And yet he was asleep. Suddenly, the air became cold. He saw a terrible dream. He was at Fagin’s house again. There sat Fagin at the table, pointing at him and talking to another man in a black coat.

“It is Oliver, sure enough. Come away,” said Fagin.

“Yes! I wasn’t mistaken,” said the man in the black coat.

As the man said this, Oliver woke up and jumped up to his feet suddenly. Good heaven! There, at the window close

before him, stood Fagin and the man whom he had seen in the inn! They were like a flash before Oliver's eyes. The next moment they were gone. But they had recognized him for sure. Oliver called for help loudly. When the dwellers of the house ran up to Oliver, they found him very pale and scared.

"Fagin! Fagin!" cried Oliver.

Dr Losberne, who had heard Oliver's story, understood him at once.

"What direction did he run away?" asked the doctor.

"That," answered Oliver, pointing out the way the man had run away.

Dr Losberne ran out of the house at his full speed. Harry Maylie and Mr Giles followed him in his chase, too. They did not stop for a long time. But the search was all in vain. There were not even the traces of footsteps on the ground. They stood now on a high hill, from which they could see anything for three or two miles. But they could not see anybody.

"It must be a dream," said Dr Losberne, when he came back home with his companions.

"No. I saw them both, as plainly as I see you now," said Oliver.

The gentlemen looked at each other in doubt. They believed Oliver, but still there were no traces of footsteps left on the ground near the house. On the next day, they searched the place once again. But all was in vain. The result was the same: they did not find any traces of footsteps. After a few days, they forgot the accident and did not talk about it anymore. Meanwhile, Rose was quickly recovering. She could go out of the room and walk with her family in the garden. One day, Dr Losberne, Mr Giles, and Harry Maylie decided to come back to London. When a carriage stopped by the gate, Harry asked Oliver to come up to him kindly.

"Oliver, I will not be at home for some time," said Harry. "I want you to write to me once in two weeks. I would like to know how my mother and Miss Rose are. Will you write me?"

"Of course! I will be proud to do it," replied Oliver gladly.

As Harry said this, he shook Oliver's hand and took his seat in the carriage. The next moment the carriage drove away rapidly and soon was out of sight. Mrs Maylie, Rose, and Oliver looked after the carriage for a while and then entered the house silently.

Chapter 11

A Talk Between Mr And Mrs Bumble And Mr Monks

Mr Bumble sat in the workhouse parlour, reading a newspaper very seriously. Now a great change happened in the position of his affairs. His hat and coat looked more respectful and fashionable. Mr Bumble was no longer a beadle. He married Mrs Corney (the woman who was next to the old nurse when she died) and was master of the workhouse. After some time, Mr Bumble got up and went out of the workhouse into the street. He walked through many streets in a respectful manner. All of a sudden, it began to rain heavily. Mr Bumble entered quickly one of the inns and sat at a table. There sat a tall man at the neighbouring table, with a black hat and long coat. He watched Mr Bumble attentively for a moment. Mr Bumble looked askew at the stranger, too. When their glances met, the stranger said at last:

"I have seen you before, I think. You were a beadle in the workhouse, weren't you?"

"I was a beadle before. Now I am a master of the workhouse," said Mr Bumble.

The stranger stood up, come up to Mr Bumble's table, and sat opposite him.

"Now listen to me," said the stranger. "I want some information from you. Carry your memory back. The scene was twelve years ago, in the workhouse. A boy was born there at night."

"Many boys were born twelve years ago," said Mr Bumble.

"I talk of one boy," said the stranger. "A thin boy who was apprenticed to a coffin-maker and then ran away to London."

"You mean Oliver!" said Mr Bumble. "Oliver Twist! I remember him, of course. He is the worst boy I had ever seen in my life."

"I don't want to hear about him," said the stranger. "I have heard enough of him. I want to know about the woman who had nursed his mother. Where is she?"

"She died last winter," answered Mr Bumble.

The stranger was very surprised at this answer. He was thoughtful for a while. But Mr Bumble was a cunning and curious man. He remembered the night when Mrs Sally had died very well. He knew the woman who had nursed Mrs Sally before her death. It was actually Mrs Corney, his wife. He told the stranger about Mrs Corney with a cunning smile.

"How can I find her?" asked the stranger.

"I can help you," said Mr Bumble.

"Come tomorrow to this place, at nine o'clock in the evening. My name is Monks," said the stranger, writing down an address on a newspaper which lay on the table.

With these words, the stranger stood up and went away without a word. Mr Bumble sat motionless for a moment. Then he went out of the inn and came home quickly. His curiosity knew no boundaries. He told his wife about the stranger in the inn and his request. They waited for the next day impatiently. Luckily, the next day passed quite rapidly. And then the evening came. Mr and Mrs Bumble took a carriage and went towards a poor town a few miles away from London. The town stood near a long river. They were both wrapped in old clothes, so as not to draw people's attention very much. Mr Bumble carried a small lantern in his hand, and Mrs Corney walked beside him carefully. The place looked gloomy and dangerous. All the houses were old and poor, and only homeless people and criminals could live there. Shortly, they stopped before a ruinous building. It was an abandoned factory.

"Hello, there! Wait a minute. I will lead you inside," said a voice from above.

Mr Bumble looked up and saw a man looking out of a window. Then the man disappeared and the window closed. Soon Monks opened the door, near which they stood, and led them inside. They were in a dark and cold room. There was only one small candle in the room. Mr Bumble felt very uncomfortable and scared at the time. He was silent.

"So this is the woman you told me about?" asked Monks.

"Yes," answered Mr Bumble.

"So you were with that old nurse the night she died. She told you something," said Monks, looking at Mrs Corney.

"Well, firstly, I would like to have some money for this information," said Mrs Corney cunningly.

Monks seemed angry to hear that. But then he gave a purse of coins to Mrs Corney sullenly. Mrs Corney was satisfied when she saw the purse in her hand, which contained twenty-five pounds.

"Well," said Mrs Corney, "when this woman that we called old Sally, died, she and I were alone. I stood alone beside her bed. She spoke of a young woman who had given a birth to a boy in the workhouse. The boy was called Oliver Twist. The old nurse had robbed the dead mother when she lay in her bed. Old Sally has taken something from the dead woman which she had prayed to keep for the child. It was something that she wore all the time. The old nurse clasped it in her hand when she died."

"What was it?" asked Monks.

"There," said Mr Corney, taking a small bag from her pocket.

Monks took the bag and opened it impatiently. There was a little gold locket. The word 'Agnes' was engraved on the inside.

"And this is all?" asked Monks.

"Yes," replied Mrs Bumble.

Mr Bumble drew a long breath. He seemed to be glad that the story was over at last.

"What do you suppose to do with this information?" asked Mr Bumble.

"This story will not be used against you or me," said Monks. "Be careful! Don't move a step forward, or your life is over!"

With these words, he suddenly pulled a large iron door on the floor which opened close at Mr Bumble's feet. Mr and Mrs Bumble stepped back in fear.

"Don't be afraid. Come closer," said Monks.

They come up to the hole in the floor carefully. The dirty water was running rapidly below the factory. Monks looked at

the gold locket for a while and then dropped it into the stream below. It fell down with a loud splash and was gone at once.

"Now this story must be a secret between us," said Monks.

"You may trust us. We will never tell anybody about this secret," said Mr Bumble.

"I am glad to hear it. Now go away from here as fast as you can!" said Monks.

Mr and Mrs Bumble went out of the old factory without looking back. They walked at an incredible speed. The married couple was very scared. Monks looked after them from the window above. When the couple was out of sight, he closed the window and went back to the room he has just left.

Chapter 12

A Strange Talk

On the evening when the three persons met in the factory in the last chapter, Mr Sikes awakened from a long sleep and asked what time of night it was. The room in which Mr Sikes asked this question was old and dusty. It was lighted only by a small window in the roof. The robber was lying on the bed, wrapped in his long coat and a ragged blanket. He looked ill and pale. He hadn't shaven for a week or so. The dog sat beside him, watching his master attentively all the time. Nancy was sitting by the window silently. She was very pale and worried.

"It is only seven o'clock. How do you feel tonight, Bill?" said Nancy.

"I am very weak. Help me to get up now. Right now!" answered Sikes.

Sikes was sick, but his illness did not change his temper.

"So many nights I have been nursing you, as if you had been a child. I think you could be kind to me," said Nancy.

"Well, then," said Sikes, taking Nancy by the hand and trying to get up slowly. "Women are always right. Thank you for your help."

At that moment Fagin entered the room without knocking at the door. Jack and Charles Bates followed him into the room. Fagin put some packages of food on the table and then came up to Sikes.

"Why did you leave me here in this state for three weeks, like a sick rat in the hole?" asked Sikes angrily.

"Just hear him, boys! We brought him all these tasty things and he talks so angrily!" said Fagin with a smile on his face.

Sikes did not say anything. He was deeply offended.

"I was away from London for two weeks," said Fagin. "I could not come to you. Don't be angry with me. I did not forget you, Bill. Never."

"It is all very well, but I need some money from you. I have no money in my pocket," said Sikes.

"Well, I will send Jack to you tonight. He will bring you some money," said Fagin.

Shortly, Sikes fell asleep soundly. Fagin sent the boys out on some errand and sat down by the warm fire as usual. Nancy sat at the table with her hands folded, showing no interest in anything around her. After some time, there was a soft knock at the door. The next moment Monks came in quickly into the room. Fagin greeted him in a friendly manner. Nancy looked at the stranger indifferently.

"Any news?" asked Fagin.

"Great news," answered Monks.

Nancy looked at the stranger more attentively than before. She was very curious at the time. Fagin told Monks to go out of the room for a short talk. When the sound of their footsteps stopped, the girl came up to the door and began to listen with breathless interest. She listened to them secretly for a while and then sat at the table again, as if she had not stood up at all. Fagin came in and looked at Nancy suspiciously.

"What have you done while I was talking to him?" asked Fagin.

"Nothing. I was sitting here all the time," answered Nancy.

"Good," said Fagin. "I will go back to my house now. Stay here with Sikes and look after him as well as you can."

When Fagin went out of the room, Nancy sat motionless for some time. Then she left the house and began to cry bitterly in the street. She was scared and confused at the same time. She walked through the streets without knowing where to go for a few hours. As evening came, she came back to the old house and sat by the fire. Her fear and excitement increased greatly. Her cheeks were unusually pale. There was a strange fire in her eyes. Sikes lay in his bed and was very weak from the fever. By and by, he fell asleep as soundly as a child. Nancy was very desperate at that moment.

"It may be too late. I must go at once!" said Nancy to herself.

She quickly took her shawl and went out of the house, looking fearfully around all the time. It was ten o'clock in the evening. She walked quickly to the more wealthy part of London. The streets were mostly silent and empty. Soon she stopped near a hotel in a quiet street. The clock struck eleven. She looked around again and then entered the hotel carefully.

"What do you want here?" asked an old woman out of a door behind her.

"I must see Miss Maylie. I have a short message for her," answered Nancy.

The old woman looked at her suspiciously for a moment. Then she ran upstairs to inform Mrs Maylie that there was a visitor who wanted to talk to her straight away. After a few minutes, Nancy was told that Miss Maylie waited for her upstairs. Nancy entered the room shamefully. She was ashamed of her poor clothes and outer appearance in general. She was the miserable companion of thieves and the fallen outcast of respectable society. Miss Maylie looked at the poor girl attentively. She did not judge Nancy according to her appearance.

"Sit down. Tell me why you wished to see me," said Rose Maylie kindly.

"Let me stand," said Nancy. "I am going to put my life in your hands. I am the girl who dragged little Oliver back to Fagin's house on the night he went out from the house in Pentonville."

"You!" said Rose in surprise.

"Yes," said Nancy. "I am a bad woman that lives among the thieves. I have not known any better life from my childhood. I ran away tonight in order to talk to you seriously. Do you know a man called Monks?"

"No," answered Rose.

"But he knows you," said Nancy. "He knows you are here. I overheard him today in the morning. This is how I found you here. He made Oliver commit the robbery in your house that night. One day, Monks saw him accidentally on the street. He recognized him at once. There was a bargain between Fagin and Monks for a certain sum. Fagin wanted Oliver to become a thief of his gang."

"And what happened then?" asked Rose.

"Fagin gave Monks his money for the bargain," replied Nancy. "Because Oliver had not become the thief of his gang. After that, Monks said he knew who the boy was. He said that the only proof of the boy's identity lay at the bottom of the river. Moreover, he said that Oliver was his brother!"

"His brother!" cried Rose in astonishment.

"These were his words," said Nancy. "And more. Then he spoke of you and the other lady. He knows that Oliver lives with you. It is growing late now. I have to go back without suspicion."

"But what should I do now?" asked Rose.

"You must find some kind gentleman that will hear this story as a secret, and advice you what to do," answered Nancy.

"But where can I find you again when it is necessary?" asked Rose.

"Every Sunday night, from eleven until twelve o'clock I will walk on London Bridge if I am alive," replied Nancy.

Thus speaking, Nancy turned to the door and went away without another word. Rose sank into the chair, trying to collect her thoughts. Nancy's words touched her heart greatly. They wanted to remain in London only for three days. It was now midnight of the first day. What could she do now? And who could give her a wise advice? Rose was very disturbed by these thoughts for a long time. She passed a sleepless and anxious night. The next morning, Oliver entered the room quickly. He breathed very hard.

"What happened, Oliver?" asked Rose in alarm.

"Oh! I saw him at last!" said Oliver. "The gentleman who was so kind to me once. And you should know that I have told you the truth! He was going out of a carriage and going into a house. He did not see me. Mr Giles was next to me at that moment. He asked a servant near the house whether Mr Brownlow lived there or not. He said he did. I am going there directly! I have his address on a piece of paper."

Rose read the address attentively. She knew the place very well.

"Quickly! I will take you there directly," said Rose.

In less than five minutes they were in the carriage on their way to Mr Brownlow's house. When they arrived there, Rose asked a servant to see Mr Brownlow on very urgent business. The servant soon returned and told them to follow him into an upper room. Rose asked Oliver to wait behind the door for a while and came in with a serious look. Mr Brownlow sat in an armchair, with his hands clasped on the top of a thick stick. Mr Grimwig sat beside him with a newspaper on his knees. Rose introduced herself to the two gentlemen quickly.

"You once showed a great kindness to my young friend. His name is Oliver Twist," said Rose.

Mr Brownlow and his friend were very surprised to hear this name.

"Miss Maylie, once I had a very good opinion of Oliver. But one day he had escaped with my money…" said Mr Brownlow.

"A bad boy! A thief!" said Mr Grimwig.

"Do not mind my friend, Miss Maylie. Please, tell me what happened to Oliver? How is he?" said Mr Brownlow.

Rose told the gentleman of all that had happened to Oliver since he left his house. Mr Brownlow listened to her very carefully. When the story was finished, he thanked Rose for all that she had done for Oliver.

“He is waiting behind the door,” said Rose.

Just then Mr Brownlow opened the door, came up to Oliver, and hugged him tightly. Both of them were very happy to see each other after such a long time. Presently, Mr Brownlow sent Oliver to the old nurse who had nursed him when he had a fever. As Oliver left the room, Rose told Mr Brownlow a full story of her talk with Nancy. Mr Brownlow was very surprised at the story he has just heard from Rose. He told Rose that he would come to their hotel at eight o’clock that evening. When their talk was over, Rose and Oliver returned to their hotel joyfully. There they met Dr Losberne in the hall, who came to visit them without warning. That day, Rose told him Nancy’s story in detail. Dr Losberne decided to help Oliver as well. Mr Brownlow arrived at the hotel at eight o’clock and they all sat at the dinner table anxiously. Oliver had dinner earlier and was in another room, busy with his studies and tasks.

“What should we do then?” said Dr Losberne at the table.

“First, we must find out who Oliver’s parents were,” said Mr Brownlow.

“Ah, I almost forgot that,” said the doctor. “I think we must also put these thieves in prison. The police may hang a few of them. This will serve them right!”

“Very good idea,” said Mr Brownlow. “But we must think of Oliver’s safety as well. We cannot put all the thieves in prison. Some of them would remain in London and would have revenge on Oliver afterwards.”

“Then we have to catch Monks when he is not surrounded by these thieves,” said the doctor. “Nancy can tell us where we can find Monks. We must wait till Sunday. Meantime, we must remain very careful. I will ask Harry Maylie to come to London and help us with this dangerous matter."

"That's right. I will ask Mr Grimwig for help as well," said Mr Brownlow.

"So we will stay in London and solve the mystery of Oliver's parents," said Rose.

With these words, the council was over for the present.

Chapter 13

Oliver's Old Acquaintance Becomes A Thief

On the night when Nancy went to Miss Maylie, two persons had just come to London by the Great North Road. They were a man and a woman. The man was thin and pale. The woman was young and worried. They were married for a few months. They came to London for the first time. They had a heavy luggage and a parcel wrapped in a handkerchief. Thus they walked along the dusty road. The woman turned to her husband tiredly. Her husband's name was Noah Claypole.

"Where will we stop for the night, Noah?" asked Charlotte.

"Near, I hope," replied Noah.

So they walked through the crowded streets for some time until they stopped in front of a small inn. They entered the inn and sat at the table, pulling their luggage closer to them. There was nobody in the inn but Fagin, sitting in the corner and reading a dirty newspaper. Noah asked the landlord for a room and a good dinner. The landlord nodded in agreement and took their luggage upstairs without a word. Presently, a good dinner was served and the couple began to eat with pleasure. While they were eating their dinner, Fagin listened to them attentively in the dark corner. Fagin liked Noah Claypole because he looked like a thief.

"So I want to be a gentleman," said Noah to his wife. "No more old coffins in my life! I will become a thief. I will rob pockets, houses, and banks! You will help me, of course. I never saw such a deceitful woman as you, Charlotte. We must find some thief band at first."

"It sounds nice, Noah," said Charlotte.

At that moment Fagin raised from the table in the corner and came up to Noah and his wife.

"The weather is good today," said Fagin. "You seem to be a clever fellow, sir. You are a new comer, I think. London is a nice city. But if you want to be rich, you always need to empty some pockets, houses or banks."

Noah fell back in his chair and looked at Fagin with terror on his face.

"Don't be afraid," said Fagin. "I heard you by chance. It was lucky it was only me. I am a thief. I liked you and your companion. I can help you. I will put you in the right way. You will be taught by me in the best manner. The conditions are simple: you will live like a gentleman in my house with free food and drinks. But half of what you and your wife steal will be mine."

"I am so lucky to meet you here!" said Noah. "We will work with you with pleasure. What can I do in the beginning?"

"Well," said Fagin, "My friend wants somebody who would spy one girl. Easy work, I think. You can do it."

"Agreed!" said Noah.

"Tomorrow we will meet here at ten o'clock. What is your name, by the way?" said Fagin.

"I am Morris Bolter, and this is my wife Mrs Bolter," answered Noah, saying a wrong name intentionally.

"Nice to meet you then. See you tomorrow," said Fagin, leaving them with a kind smile on his face.

Noah Claypole and his wife finished their dinner and went upstairs joyfully.

The next day, Noah and his wife went to Fagin's house. There they talked about their life and robbery for hours. No doubt, they were a good company for each other.

"You have to be always careful," said Fagin to Noah. "You must remain unnoticed while you are doing your business. Otherwise, you will go to prison straight away. So you depend on me, and you must trust me all the time."

"That's right," said Noah.

"Ah, my best robber, Jack Dawkins, was taken from me yesterday," said Fagin. "The officer saw him trying to steal a silver box. He was worth fifty silver boxes! He is in police office now. I hope we will have him back again after six weeks if they don't get any evidence. That's why you have to be always careful, my dear friend."

"I am so sorry to hear that," said Noah.

Just then Charles Bates entered the room suddenly. He looked very distressed.

"It is over. The police has found the evidence against Jack," said Charles Bates.

Fagin was surprised to hear that. He was thoughtful for a while.

"Never mind, Charles," said Fagin. "They will keep him in prison like a gentleman. What a glory to be taken to prison at such age! Anyway, somebody has to go to the police office and find out everything about Jack."

"Right you are!" said Noah.

"You will go, Morris Bolter," said Fagin, turning to Noah with a serious look. "Nobody knows you there. You look like a gentleman."

Mr Bolter agreed to undertake an expedition unwillingly. He listened to Fagin's directions attentively and then went out of the old house. Noah Claypole, or Morris Bolter as he had called himself, presently reached the police office without attracting anybody's attention. He entered a dirty room which was overcrowded and smelly. Noah looked eagerly about him for Jack Dawkins. By and by, he saw a young boy walking with an officer to another room of the prison. He looked exactly as Fagin had described him to Noah just an hour ago.

"Who is it?" asked one of the magistrates, looking at Jack Dawkins scornfully.

"A pocket robber, sir," answered the officer. "His guilt has been absolutely proven by witnesses. He will be sent to prison soon."

The magistrate nodded in approval and went away without saying a word.

"I will not be frightened! You will pay for this, all of you!" said Jack, looking at the officer angrily.

With these words, Jack Dawkins was led off by the officer into the yard. Noah saw everything he needed to see in the police office. He walked back to Fagin's house as quickly as he could.

***

Despite her cunning, Nancy could hardly keep herself calm and quiet. She knew that Fagin and Sikes trusted her completely.

But they had led her down into the abyss of crime and misery, whence there was no escape. Still, there were times when she felt some doubts. Anyway, she kept her secret very well. She knew what she would do despite all her mental struggles. She grew pale and thin within a few days. She did not mind what was happening around her. She was silent all the time. It was Sunday night, and the bell of the nearest church struck ten. Sikes and Fagin were talking next to her in the room. The bell struck eleven. Nancy got up, put on her bonnet, and walked to the door.

"Nancy! Where are you going at this time of night?" asked Sikes.

"I don't know where," answered Nancy. "Not far. I'm not well. I want to walk a bit."

"No. You will not go anywhere. Sit down," said Sikes.

"I will go!" said Nancy.

"No! You will stay here!" cried Sikes.

The next moment Sikes took her by the hand and dragged her into another room. Then he closed the door with a key and sat in front of Fagin again. They continued to talk as if nothing had happened. The bell struck twelve. Fagin took up his hat and said good-night to Sikes in a friendly manner. As he walked away, he opened the room and looked at Nancy attentively. She looked very worried and angry. Fagin had some suspicions about her, because her behaviour was too unusual and different. Thus Fagin walked towards his house, thinking of Nancy and her strange behaviour. Her changed manners, her wish to walk at night alone, and an absolute indifference to the interests of the gang planted many doubts in his mind. Fagin decided to find out everything without delay. He knew how he could do that. The next morning, he told Noah to sit beside him for a serious talk.

"Bolter," said Fagin, "I want you to do something for me. There is no danger in it. All you need is to spy a young woman."

"I can do that very well," said Noah.

"You have to tell me where she goes," said Fagin, "who she sees, and, if possible, what she says. Bring me back as much information as you can. I will give you one pound for this work. She is one of us. She has found some new friends and I must know who they are. I will tell you when to do it. Just be ready."

"I will wait for your directions then," said Noah.

Chapter 14

Fatal Consequences

Six nights passed quickly. It was Sunday at last. Fagin described Nancy to Noah and told him to wait near the old house, where Nancy and Sikes lived at the present. It was eleven o'clock. The door was closed. But presently it opened softly and Nancy went out of the house, looking carefully around her all the time. Then she began to walk in the street in a hurry. Noah walked as near as he could, and kept on the opposite side of the street. Nancy looked nervously around twice or trice. The spy kept the same distance and followed the girl secretly. Soon Nancy reached London Bridge and stopped before two persons, an old gentleman and a young lady. Noah stopped before the bridge in the shadow of a tree. They stood there in silence for a moment. A mist hung over the river, rendering indistinct the dark buildings on the banks. Midnight had come upon the crowded city. Nancy looked around nervously for a few times.

"Not here. I am afraid to speak to you here. Let's come down the steps a little," said Nancy.

As she said these words and showed with her hand the direction in which she wished them to walk, they all went down the steps silently. These steps were a part of the bridge, they consisted of three flights. Nancy and her companions stood below the end of the second flight, and Noah reached the other one secretly. There he was absolutely unseen by Nancy and her companions. He was very curious to hear the reasons for their secret talk. He drew himself straight against the wall and began to listen attentively.

"Why have you brought us to this strange place?" asked the old gentleman.

"I was afraid to speak to you there," answered Nancy. "I don't know why, but I feel very scared. I have horrible thoughts of death…"

"You were not here last Sunday night," said the young lady.

"I couldn't come," said Nancy. "They kept me in the room by force. But tonight no one knows I am here. Sikes was alone in the house. I gave him a drink of laudanum before I came away. He is asleep now."

"Good," said Mr Brownlow. "Now listen to me. Miss Rose told me the whole story, and to some other friends whom we can trust completely. I believe you without doubts. We must find Monks. But if he cannot be found, you must tell us where Fagin lives."

"I will find Monks for you," said Nancy.

Then Nancy began to talk in a very low voice. Noah could only hear the name of the inn in which Monks stayed most of the time. After that, Nancy explained the location of the place and the hour on which Monks usually visited it.

"He is tall," said Nancy. "He walks quickly, looking over his shoulder. His face is dark, like his hair and eyes. His lips are often pale. Moreover, there is red mark on his throat."

"You helped us very much. What can we do for you?" said Mr Brownlow.

"Nothing," replied Nancy. "Nobody can help me. I have no hope. I am chained to my old life. I hate it now, but I cannot leave it. I must go home."

"They will kill you there!" said Rose Maylie.

"I must go home, Miss Maylie. To such a home where I have raised as a thief," said Nancy.

Just then the voices stopped and the sound of the retreating feet was audible in the distance. The young lady and her companion soon appeared on the bridge again. They went down the street without looking back. Noah Claypole went away, too. He went to Fagin's house as fast as his legs would carry him. Noah arrived at Fagin's house pretty soon. Fagin was sitting at the table sleepily. He was pale and thoughtful. His face was turned toward a burning candle that stood on the table by his side. When he saw Noah entering the room, he stood up and looked at him seriously. Noah told him the whole story about Nancy without delay. Fagin was beside himself with anger. He hated the girl who had dared to tell their secrets to strangers. He was deeply disappointed. The fear of prison, ruin, and death were all mixed together. He sent one of the thieves to call for Sikes immediately. Then he waited for Sikes impatiently. Presently, Sikes came in with an anxious look.

"At last!" said Fagin.

Soon they sat against each other, face to face. Fagin's lips shook violently. His face was fully changed by the emotions that had come over him. His anger was so great that his power of speech was gone for a moment.

"Well, what would you do if some of us had told the strangers all about us?" asked Fagin with a furious smile.

"I would kill him! Whoever it was, I would kill him at once!" answered Sikes.

Fagin was silent for a while. Then he asked Noah to tell Sikes of everything he has seen and heard that night. Noah did so with great pleasure. Sikes was shocked and angry at the same time. He jumped to his feet and ran to the door.

"Bill, stop!" said Fagin when Sikes ran up to the door. "Don't be too violent! Think well before you do something!"

Sikes made no reply. He pulled the door and ran into the silent street quickly. He was running towards his house without one pause. He did not see anything around himself. His anger was beyond limits. By and by, he reached his house and opened the door softly with a key. He walked upstairs slowly and entered the room where the girl was lying in her bad. He roused her from her sleep with a strong push.

"Get up!" cried Sikes.

"Bill, why do you look at me like that?" asked the girl in surprise.

The thief looked at her angrily for a while.

"One thief followed you to the bridge tonight. Every word you said was heard by him," said Sikes.

"Bill, just listen to me first!" cried Nancy. "You cannot kill me now! The gentleman and the young lady are very kind. They can save you from prison. Let's leave this dreadful place and become decent people! It is never too late to change our life…"

Sikes seized his pistol in a moment. Then he fired without mercy. Nancy fell dead on the floor silently. The murder stepped back and sat down paralyzed with terror. This was the worst action committed that night in London. Soon the morning came as usual. The sun shone brightly. It lighted up the room in which the murdered woman lay. Sikes had not moved in his chair. He was afraid to move. Shortly, he stood up and threw his pistol into the fire. Then he washed himself and his clothes. All this time, he never turned to the corpse on the floor. When he was ready, he moved toward the door and left the house with his dog. He felt calmer outside of the house. He walked for hours, not knowing where to go or what to do. Where could he go? Where could he get some food and water? Hendon. That was a good place for him.

Chapter 15

The Pursuit And Escape

When he reached Hendon, all the people seemed to look at him with suspicion. He walked for miles without a stop. Morning and noon passed in this manner. It was nine o'clock at night. At last, he entered a small inn and ordered some dinner for himself. He and his dog ate greedily for some time. Then he sat silent and unnoticed in the corner, and had almost fallen asleep with tiredness. Presently, he woke up and went out of the inn carefully. Nobody followed him. He walked through the street, avoiding the light of the lamps and the crowded places. Soon he saw a post carriage in the street. Two men were talking to each other near the post carriage. Sikes could hear them very well as he passed them by.

"Anything new up in London?" asked one of the men.

"Well, I heard some talk of a murder," answered another man. "It was a very dreadful murder. A young woman was shot in an old house. The police try to find the murderer now. They think he went to Birmingham. The whole country knows about the murder."

"Oh, it is so terrible!" said the man.

Sikes was shocked by what he had just heard. He did not know where to go next. At last, he decided to go to St Albans. He walked in the darkness of the streets, looking back all the time. He was in agony of fear and despair. That night, he found some old, abandoned house and hid there with his dog. The consciousness of crime never left his mind. Many terrible visions seemed to come to his mind one by one. Nevertheless, he had a long but uneasy sleep. The next day, he resolved to go back to London. He knew that the police were looking for

him in Birmingham. That is why it was dangerous to go to Birmingham. Thus he began his journey back to London. His dog walked tiredly behind his master. All of a sudden, the dog stopped and refused to follow his master.

"Come back!" cried Sikes to his dog.

The dog wagged his tail but did not move. Sikes called him again. The dog looked at his master and then ran away as fast as he could. Sikes sat down and waited that his dog would return soon. But the dog did not come back. Sikes continued his journey alone sadly.

***

That very day, Mr Brownlow knocked softly at the door of his own house. The door was opened carefully by one of his servants. As the door was opened, two strong men led a man into the house, holding him tightly by the hands. This man was Monks. They walked into a room without speaking.

"Why I was kidnapped in the street and brought here by these men?" asked Monks.

"I asked them to do it," said Mr Brownlow. "Sit down. We need to talk seriously. If you refuse to talk, I will give you to the police at once."

Monks looked at the old gentleman anxiously. Mr Brownlow told the two men to leave them for a while. The men did so, and Mr Brownlow and Monks were left alone together.

"Good treatment from my father's old friend," said Monks.

"Yes, I was your father's friend," said Mr Brownlow. "I was in love with your aunt at the time. I wanted to marry her... But she died so suddenly. And now you are here in my house, Edward Leeford."

"Well, what do you want from me?" asked Monks.

"You have a brother…" said Mr Brownlow.

"I have no brother. I was an only child," said Monks.

"Fifteen years ago, when you were eleven years old, your mother died," said Mr Brownlow. "Your father was very distressed. But he had a good friend. He was a naval officer who had two beautiful daughters."

"What is this to me?" asked Monks.

"Listen to me attentively," said Mr Brownlow. "One of his daughters was in love with your father. But this love was full of grief and sorrow. One of the relatives of your family after his death in Italy had left to your father a lot of money. Your father had to go to Italy immediately for this reason. Unfortunately, he was taken ill there. So the whole property fell to your mother and you. Your father came to me before he went to Italy."

"I never heard of that," said Monks.

"He came to me and left me a picture," continued Mr Brownlow. "It was a picture of his friend's daughter whom he loved so much. He told me the whole story about their secret love. Her name was Agnes. Then he went to Italy, promising to write and tell me about all that would happen to him and Agnes. Alas! I never saw him again. He died in Italy. Soon afterwards, Agnes gave birth to a boy, your brother. He was a weak and neglected child. I met this boy by chance twelve years after his birth. I helped this poor boy when he was seized by fever. He remained in my house for a month or so. I noticed a strong resemblance to the picture that your father had given to me. I wanted to find out more about this story, but the child was kidnapped in the street by the thieves like you."

Monks looked very surprised and confused.

"Your mother and father were dead," continued Mr Brownlow, "and I knew that I alone could solve the mystery. I heard that you were in West Indies. I went there at once, but you had left it months before. You had been in London, but no one could tell where. I returned to London. And, at last, I have found you. I have learned the whole story. Your mother had destroyed your father's will. This will told of the child who was the result of his sad and secret love. You hated your brother from the very beginning. You have thrown a locket into the river which belonged to Oliver's mother. You have killed a woman who knew something of this secret story…"

"No, no!" cried Monks. "I have not killed her! Another robber has done it! He will be found soon! His dog has been seen today, walking about some small town close to London. There is a reward of a hundred pounds for anyone who would deliver him alive to the police office."

"Well, remain here till I return. It is your only hope of safety," said Mr Brownlow.

The old gentleman left the room immediately. Monks remained in the room alone. His mind was busy with many different thoughts.

***

Near to that part of the Thames, where the buildings on the banks are dirtiest and oldest, there exists the strangest place that is hidden in London. To reach this place, a visitor has to walk through many muddy and narrow streets. In such a neighbourhood, stands Jacob's Island, surrounded by a muddy pond on every side of it. In Jacob's Island, the houses are roofless and empty. The windows are broken and the doors are falling into the streets. The houses have no owners. Poor people can enter them and live there without permission. In a room of one of such houses, there sat three men, looking at each other anxiously. They sat in silence. One of these men was Toby Crackit, another Mr Chitling. The third robber was a man with a dreadful scar on his face. His name was Kags. It was almost dark in the room. A small candle was burning on an old table. The terrible events of the last day had made a deep impression on three robbers. They spoke mostly in whispers.

"When did the police catch Fagin?" asked Toby Crackit.

"This afternoon, at two o'clock," said Mr Chitling. "Charles Bates and I could escape, but Fagin, Bolter and his wife were not lucky. The police caught them, too."

"The police made a ring round Fagin," said Mr Chitling. "Fagin looked all muddy and bleeding. He had no power to fight anymore. The people tried to come up to him wildly, one behind another. They were ready to tear him away! I swear"

Just then they heard a low noise on the stairs. Nobody spoke with fear. Then a door was opened and Sikes entered the room slowly. His face was covered with a bloody handkerchief. His eyes were red and his cheeks were all sunken. Not a word was spoken for some time. Soon Sikes sat down in a chair silently. At that moment Charles Bates entered the room. He looked at Sikes very angrily.

"I am not afraid of you!" cried Charles Bates. "If the police come here, I will give him up to them at once! Murderer!"

The robbers watched him in surprise. Charles Bates was beyond himself with anger. Despite his tiredness, Sikes got up and brought him to the ground with a strong blow. Sikes and the boy rolled on the floor together. Charles Bates never stopped to call for help with all his power. The next moment there were lights in the windows and the noise of hoofs rattling on the road. The footsteps became more noisily. Then came a loud knock at the door.

"Help! He is here! Break down the door!" cried Charles Bates.

Some people cried to set the house on fire, others cried to the officers to shoot him at once. Some called for a ladder, some ran with torches around the house.

"Give me a rope! I may jump into the pond and escape that way in the darkness!" cried Sikes to the robbers.

The robbers gave him the longest rope straight away. As Sikes took the rope, he ran up to the top of the house as quickly as he could. He was on the roof of the house and all the people could see him there in the light of torches. The crowd shouted loudly with excitement.

"I will give fifty pounds to the man who takes him alive!" cried the officer on a horseback.

There was another cry in the crowd. Then the door was broken and the people ran into the house madly. When the people were in the house, Sikes decided to make one last chance for his life by jumping into the pond. He fastened one end of the rope tightly around his waist and had his knife ready in the other hand to cut it. The next moment he jumped into the pond with a cry of horror. But the jump was not successful. He tied himself in knots and hung against the wall with a terrible convulsion of the legs. He was suffocated in the knots and soon

hung lifeless and silent. Presently, the people cut the rope on the roof and Sikes fell dead on the ground. The crowd became silent. The people looked at the murderer without saying a word. It was a dreadful sight.

Chapter 16

And Last

The events mentioned in the last chapter had happened two days ago. After two days, at three o'clock of the afternoon, Oliver was going to his native town in a big carriage. Mrs Maylie, Rose, and the kind doctor were with him. Mr Brownlow followed them in another carriage, with a person whose name was not mentioned to Oliver. They all travelled in silence, every one of them thought of the object which had brought them together. Oliver knew that they were going to his birth-place by a road he had never seen. He was very excited and emotional. All his thoughts ran back to the old times when he was a poor, houseless boy without a friend to help him.

"See there!" cried Oliver. "This is the place where I had lived with other orphans! I had many friends there! They were very good friends!"

"Yes, no doubt, Oliver," said Rose.

As they reached the town, it was hard to hold the boy in the carriage. He was too excited to sit still in the carriage. Soon they passed by Sowerberry's coffin shop, which looked small and old at that moment. Then they went to the workhouse – a dreadful prison of his youthful days. Everything there looked the same, as if Oliver had left it but yesterday. But now it was a pure, joyful reality. They drove to the hotel which Oliver had seen many times during his stay in the town. Mr Grimwig met them at the door with a kind smile on his face. They all entered the hotel and had a good dinner there. After that, they sat in a big room by the fire in silence. At nine o'clock, Mr Brownlow entered the room with a man whom Oliver was very surprised to see. It was the same man Oliver had seen in Fagin's house. They told him it was his brother. Monks looked at the boy with hatred and disgust. He sat down by the fire without saying a word. Mr Brownlow, who had papers in his hand, walked to a table near which Oliver and Rose were seated.

"This is a hard topic," said Mr Brownlow, turning to Monks, "but I have to tell you everything I know of Oliver. Well, Oliver is your half-brother. He is the son of your dead father and a young Agnes Fleming."

"Yes," said Monks, looking at the trembling boy scornfully. "My father died in Italy. After his death, my mother went there with me to look after his property. We found two papers on the desk. One of these papers was a letter to this girl Agnes, and the other his will. In that letter, he asked Agnes to forgive him and keep their child in a good state. He asked her also to keep the gold locket, which he had given to her."

"And what about the will?" asked Mr Brownlow.

Monks was silent for a while.

"In his will, he divided his property into two parts," said Monks. "One for my mother and me, and the other for Agnes Fleming and her child. He said that both his children were equal."

"And what happened to the will?" asked Mr Brownlow.

"My mother did what a woman should have done," answered Monks. "She burnt his will. The letter never reached Agnes. When Agnes learned about my father's death, she left her home in secret. She was pregnant at the time. She tried to hide her shame from her kind father. Her father died soon afterwards.

Agnes lived in poverty. After some time, she decided to come to London. She reached London on foot. Some old woman met her in the street and offered her help. Thus Agnes came to the workhouse where Oliver had been born. There Agnes died."

"What about the gold locket?" asked Mr Brownlow.

"I bought it from the woman who stole it from the old nurse, who stole it from dead Agnes," replied Monks.

As Monks said this, Mr Brownlow left the room and came back with Mr and Mrs Bumble.

"My dear Oliver, I am so glad to see you here! I hope you are fine," said Mr Bumble.

"Hold your tongue, fool," said Mrs Bumble.

"Do you know this person? Did you sell him a gold locket?" asked Mr Brownlow, looking at Mr Bumble.

Mr Bumble did not say anything. But when he saw Monks in the corner of the room his face changed at once. He was frightened and confused.

"I know him," said Mr Bumble. "I sold him a gold locket, which my wife had stolen from an old nurse."

Mr Brownlow asked Mr and Mrs Bumble to leave the room. They did it with great pleasure. Then Mr Brownlow turned to Monks with a serious look.

"What do you know about this young lady?" asked Mr Brownlow, pointing at Rose.

Monks was silent again.

"The father of the unhappy Agnes had two daughters," said Mr Brownlow. "Rose is the younger daughter. When her father died and Agnes left the house, Rose was given to a good family. Rose lived there and was very happy with Mrs Maylie."

"Oh, Mrs Rose is my aunt then! The kindest and best of women," cried Oliver emotionally.

"Yes, my dear," said Rose, hugging Oliver kindly.

***

The court was full of curious people. All eyes were fixed on one man – Fagin. Fagin was surrounded by people on every side. He did not move since the trial began. The judge stopped to speak and watched Fagin attentively. Then the judge left the court to take a verdict. Fagin was waiting for his verdict impatiently. He looked at the people around him sadly. He could not see the smallest sympathy with himself in their eyes. It was very silent in the court. Fagin thought of the gallows and his coming death. At last, the judge came back. The court rang with loud cries for a moment. After that, it became still and silent once again. The judge said that Fagin would die on Monday. There was a cry of joy from the people in the court. Fagin could not speak. He was as still as a marble figure. Presently, the guard led him to his cell and closed the door behind him. Fagin lay on a stone bed and thought of his past. Then came the silent night. The day passed quickly. He had one more night to live. The next day, Mr Brownlow and Oliver arrived at the prison to visit Fagin. The guard led them to Fagin's cell and stood back a few steps away from them. Fagin was sitting on his bed. His face was terrible. His mind seemed to wander to his old life all the time. He was saying to himself some meaningless words.

"Oliver! You are here! You became a real gentleman," said Fagin when he saw Oliver next to his cell.

ORDERED by
The Sherryff

AGNES

“Oh, God forgive this bad man!” said Oliver.

“Oliver, please save me!” said Fagin. “Open the door first. Then lead me outside… I can escape this dreadful place…”

“He is out of his mind, Oliver. Let’s go,” said Mr Brownlow.

And so they left the prison without speaking. The day passed quickly and the morning came. There were many people in the prison, who came there to see the death of the murderer. A dark figure stood in the center of a black stage. The terrible apparatus of death was next to him. Fagin died silently.

***

The story is almost finished. There is only a small paragraph left. Three months had passed since Fagin’s death. The property was equally divided between Oliver and Monks. Monks went with his money to America at once. After spending all his money, he became a thief again and was sent to prison. There he died soon. Mr Brownlow adopted Oliver as his son. The kind doctor returned to Chertsey and bought a good house there. He was spending his time mostly in fishing and gardening. Rose married Harry Maylie and lived with him very happily. Mr Bumble was not the master of the workhouse anymore. He and his wife became poor and began to live in the workhouse with other people. Charles Bates decided to live as an honest man. He began to work on a farm of a good family. Noah Claypole also resolved to leave his thief carrier, considering his occupation not absolutely safe and respectable. He began to work as an informer. What about Oliver Twist? Well, Mr Brownlow gave him the best education. He loved Oliver as his own son. They were very happy together.

The End

Glossary

absence – yokluk
aggravate – şiddetlendirmek
anger – öfke
apparatus – alet
apprentice – çırak
approval – onay, tasdik
ashamed – utanmış
beadle – görevli
bear – taşımak, katlanmak
beneath – altında
beside himself – kendinden geçmek
bring up – yetiştirmek
cellar – kiler
coffin – tabut
commotion – kargaşa
companions – eşlik edenler
conceal – gizlemek
conclude – sonucuna varmak
confident – kendine güvenen
confused – şaşkın
consider – düşünmek
convulsion – çırpınma
cooker – aşçı
creep – sürünmek
crust – kabuk
cunning – kurnazlık
deceive – aldatmak
dense – yoğun
departure – ayrılık
deposit – yatırmak
derisive – alaycı
desperately – umutsuzca
devote – adamak
discovery – keşif
disgust – iğrenmek
distance – mesafe
distressed – sıkıntılı
drag – sürüklemek
draw attention – dikkat çekmek
drop – düşmek
drunken – sarhoş
dwellers – sakinler, oturan
educate – eğitmek
engraved – kazınmış
evidence – kanıt
exaggeration – abartma
fabrics – kumaş
fasten – tutturmak

fever – ateş
filth – pislik
funeral - cenaze töreni
gallows – idam sehpası
gather – toplanmak
government official – devlet memuru
greedily – iştahla
greedy – aç gözlü
growl – hırlamak
gruel – yulaf lapası
hay-rick – saman yığını
housebreaking – soygun
hurl – atmak
immediate – ani
imprisonment – mahkumiyet
improve – gelişmek
in vain – nafile
indifferently – kayıtsızca
indistinct – belirsiz
inform – bilgi vermek
informer – muhbir
ingratitude – nankörlük
innocent – masum
interruption – sözünü kesme
jail – hapishane
last – sürmek
latter – bahsedilen şey, kişi
liar – yalancı
limp – topallamak
magistrate – sulh hakimi
make a bow – başıyla selamlamak
mattress – yatak
melancholy – hüzün
mention – söz etmek, anmak
miserable – sefil
mock – alay etmek
motionless – hareketsiz
neglect – ihmal etmek, ilgilenmemek
notice – farketmek
numb – uyuşmuş, hissiz
obediently – itaatkar
offence – saldırı
orphan – yetim
outcast – serseri
pale – solgun
paralyse – felç olmak
pat – okşamak
pavement – kaldırım
perplexity – şaşkınlık
polish – parlatmak
prefix – ön ek, öne eklemek
presentiment – önsezi
property – mülk

provoke – kışkırtmak
pursuit – takip
regret – pişmanlık
release – salmak, serbest bırakmak
remains – artıklar
render – çevirmek
resemblance – benzerlik
resistance – karşı koyma, direnç
resolve – karar vermek, halletmek
retreat – geri çekilmek
satisfy – tatmin olmak
scared – korkmuş
scornfully – küçümseyerek
shine (shone) – parlamak
shiver – titremek
shutters – kepenk
sneak – korkak, alçak
society – toplum
struggle – mücadele etmek, savaşmak
suffocate – boğmak
sullenly – somurtgan bir şekilde
sunken – çökmüş, çökük
survive – hayatta kalmak
suspiciously – şüpheyle
tap – hafif vurmak
tend – hizmet etmek, eğilimi olmak
threat – tehdit
tiredness – yorgunluk
trade – iş, ticaret
treachery – hıyanet
tremble – titremek
undertaker – cenazeci
uneasily – huzursuzca
unnoticeably – farkettirmeden
useless – yararsız
verdict – karar, hükum
wag – sallamak
whiskers – bıyık
whistle – ıslık çalmak
witness – tanık
workhouse – ıslahevi, düşkünler evi
wrap – sarmak
wrath – öfke, hiddet

Activities

A) TRUE OR FALSE

1) Oliver's mother couldn't see her new born child before she died. **T F**

2) Mr Bumble was a government officer who took care of all orphans in the workhouse. **T F**

3) When Oliver Twist asked for some more gruel, the cook gave him as much gruel as he wanted. **T F**

4) Noah was a good tempered boy at Oliver's age. **T F**

5) When Oliver Twist escaped from the coffin maker's shop, he travelled to London in a carriage. **T F**

6) Oliver Twist was apprenticed to a coffin maker when he was nine. **T F**

7) Bill Sikes was a tall thin young man. **T F**

8) When Mr Brownlow's close friend Mr Grimwig heard Oliver's whole life story he didn't believe it. **T F**

9) Oliver Twist robbed the big house at Chertsey and came out safe and sound. **T F**

10) Fagin was caught and sentenced to death. **T F**

B) CHOOSE THE CORRECT ANSWER

1) Oliver Twist was born ______.

A) in a hospital
B) in a workhouse
C) at home
D) in a carriage

2) The tall thin boy who Oliver met in London took him to ____.

A) a hotel
B) an old house
C) the police
D) a workhouse

3) Where was Fagin keeping the valuable goods that the boys stole for him?

A) in a safe
B) in a bank
C) in a box in a hole in the wall
D) in a box in a hole in the floor

4) When the magistrate asked Oliver what his name was ___.

A) Oliver tried to run away
B) Oliver exclaimed everything
C) Oliver fainted on the floor
D) Oliver refused to answer

5) Fagin sent ______ to the Police Station to find out what had been done to Oliver there.

A) Bill Sikes
B) Nancy
C) Charles Bates
D) Jack

6) When Oliver Twist was on his way to the book stall _____.

A) he got lost in the unknown streets
B) Nancy kidnapped him
C) he met his friends and decided to go with them
D) Mr Grimwig followed him

7) When Fagin said 'You will be the greatest man of the time.' He meant that __________.

A) Oliver would be a great man in the high society
B) Oliver would be the greatest thief
C) Oliver would be the greatest man of the time
D) Oliver would be a very good man

8) Monks took the golden locket from Mrs Corney and________.

A) dropped it into the stream that flowed under the old factory
B) wore it around his neck
C) put it into his pocket
D) took it to Mr Brownlow

9) When Nancy arrived at the Police Station to get information about Oliver, she introduced herself as Oliver Twist's ______.

A) mother
B) mother's friend
C) aunt
D) sister

10) Bill Sikes said that it would be difficult to rob the house at Chertsey because ________.

A) the dwellers were always in the house
B) it was protected very well
C) I was surrounded by high walls
D) there wasn't a place to escape after the robbery

Visit our website for the answer key.
www.mkpublications.com.tr

C) ANSWER THE QUESTIONS

1) Where was Oliver Twist born?

....

2) When did Oliver Twist's mother die?

....

3) Who stole Oliver's mother's gold locket?

....

4) What did the cook of the workhouse do when Oliver asked for some more gruel?

....

5) Where did Oliver start to work as an apprentice?

....

6) What did Oliver Twist do when Noah said some bad words for his mother?

....

7) Who did Oliver meet first when he reached London?

....

8) When did Oliver understand the whole mystery of handkerchiefs and jewels in Fagin's house?

....

9) What did the old gentleman whose handkerchief was stolen by Fagin's boys do when the officer put Oliver on the pavement?

....

10) Why did Oliver Twist lie still in bed for days in the Brownlows' house?

....

11) Who came in while Fagin was about to throw the cup in his hand at the boy's head?

....

12) What did Mr Grimwig say when he heard Oliver's story?

....

13) What did Mr Brownlow do to prove Mr Grimwig that Oliver was a trustful boy?

....

14) What did Mr Brownlow do to find Oliver?

....

15) What did the doctor who cured Oliver Twist tell the police officers who came home?

....

16) While Oliver Twist was reading a book in the small room he fell asleep. Who did he see at the window when he woke up?

....

17) Who was the stranger who met Mr Bumble in an inn and asked him some questions about Oliver Twist?

....

18) What did Monks do with the golden locket he took from Mrs Corney?

....

19) How much money did Monks pay Mrs Corney to get the golden locket?

....

20) Why did Bill Sikes kill Nancy?

....